CARL VON CLAUSEWITZ'S

ON

WAR

OTHER TITLES IN
THE **INFINITE SUCCESS** SERIES

Adam Smith's The Wealth of Nations

Benjamin Franklin's The Way to Wealth

*Charles Mackay's Extraordinary Popular Delusions
and the Madness of Crowds*

*Frank Bettger's How I Raised Myself from
Failure to Success in Selling*

George S. Clason's The Richest Man in Babylon

Karl Marx's Das Kapital

Miyamoto Musashi's The Book of Five Rings

Napoleon Hill's Think and Grow Rich

Niccolo Machiavelli's The Prince

Samuel Smiles' Self-help

Sun Tzu's The Art of War

CARL VON CLAUSEWITZ'S

ON
WAR

A MODERN-DAY INTERPRETATION
OF A STRATEGY CLASSIC
BY ANDREW HOLMES

First published in 2010 by
Infinite Ideas Limited
36 St Giles
Oxford, OX1 3LD
United Kingdom
www.infideas.com

A CIP catalogue record for this book is available from the British Library

ISBN 978–1–906821–35–7

Brand and product names are trademarks or registered trademarks of their
respective owners.

Designed and typeset by Cylinder
Printed in Great Britain

BRILLIANT IDEAS

INTRODUCTION 1

1. WAR AS AN ACT OF HUMAN INTERCOURSE 3

2. THE KNOWLEDGE REQUIRED IN WAR IS VERY SIMPLE ... 5

3. THEORY SHOULD BE STUDY, NOT DOCTRINE 7

4. ON HISTORICAL EXAMPLES 9

5. WAR IS NEVER AN ISOLATED ACT 11

6. THE EFFECT OF THE POLITICAL AIM ON THE MILITARY
   OBJECTIVE 13

7. THE CHARACTER OF CONTEMPORARY WARFARE 15

8. GENERAL SURVEY 17

9. RELATIONSHIP BETWEEN THE BRANCHES OF THE
   SERVICE 19

10. THE ORDER OF BATTLE 21

11. BASE OF OPERATIONS 23

12. LINES OF COMMUNICATION 25

13. MAINTENANCE AND SUPPLY 27

14. METHOD AND ROUTINE 29

15. TERRAIN 31

16. FORTRESSES 33

17. BILLETS 35

18. MORAL FACTORS 37

19. ON MILITARY GENIUS 39

20. THE THIRST FOR FAME AND HONOUR 41

21. ON DANGER 43

22. BOLDNESS 45

23. PERSEVERANCE 47

24. CUNNING 49

25. SURPRISE 51

26. MILITARY VIRTUES OF THE ARMY 53

27. OTHER EMOTIONAL FACTORS 55

28. THE NATURE OF BATTLE TODAY 57

29. MUTUAL AGREEMENT TO FIGHT 59

30. ADVANCED GUARDS AND OUTPOSTS 61

31. OPERATIONAL USE OF ADVANCED CORPS 63

32. CONCENTRATION OF FORCES IN SPACE 65

33. UNIFICATION OF FORCES IN TIME 67

34. THE STRATEGIC RESERVE 69

35. MAXIMUM USE OF FORCE 71

36. RELATIVE STRENGTH 73

37. SUPERIORITY OF NUMBERS 75

38. THE DYNAMIC LAW 77

39. WAR PLANS 79

40. CRITICAL ANALYSIS 81

41. FRICTION IN WAR 83

42. INTELLIGENCE IN WAR 85

43. THE BATTLE: ITS DECISION 87

44. DURATION OF THE ENGAGEMENT 89

45. THE EFFECTS OF VICTORY 91

46. STRATEGIC MEANS OF EXPLOITING VICTORY 93

47. THE COMMAND OF HEIGHTS 95

48. THE KEY TO THE COUNTRY 97

49. TYPES OF RESISTANCE 99

50. THE CHARACTER OF STRATEGIC DEFENCE 101

51. RETREAT AFTER A LOST BATTLE 103

52. RETREAT TO THE INTERIOR OF THE COUNTRY 105

REFERENCE MATERIAL 107

INDEX 109

INTRODUCTION

Typically, the only people who get to read Carl von Clausewitz are military historians and budding army cadets. The simple reason for this is that they have to; it's part of their training.

Von Clausewitz's book *On War* is a classic – of that, there is no doubt – but we must remember that it was never truly finished. In fact, his wife published the work in 1832, a year after he died, so he didn't even get the chance to show off to his friends and family.

Reading this volume which is divided into eight books, or should I say wading through, is difficult and it seems very little, if any, editing was done on the manuscript prior to publication. I am not alone in this thinking as many of those who picked up *On War* when it was first published were of the same opinion. And if only to prove how unpopular a read it was, it didn't even exhaust the first print run of 1,500 copies after 20 years. But to be fair, von Clausewitz had every intention not only of finishing the book but also reviewing, revising and updating before sending it to his publisher (as all good authors should, of course), so we should cut the guy some slack. I am also convinced that his wife and indeed the publisher had no idea what he was writing about, so just published whatever there was. Still, von Clausewitz was a bit of a genius and *On War* retains its pre-eminence in military thinking.

Von Clausewitz began jotting down his thoughts, observations and ideas about war while still in his early twenties and throughout his military career in the Prussian army he continued to add to these notes. He served in a number of major campaigns and his thinking was heavily influenced by the actions of Napoleon and his experiences during the Napoleonic Wars. Although von Clausewitz served in the army and was even a prisoner of war for a time, he was really a thinker who studied war to a depth that no one else had ever done before. And he studied it to such a degree that many failed to see the gems hidden deep inside the detail. Fortunately, enough people did read the work, and with a bit of editing, his observations, advice and genius shone through. As a result, *On War* has heavily influenced military thinking ever since.

Creating a modern-day, business-focused interpretation has been an interesting challenge. On first blush you might think that war is war and business is business, but trawling through von Clausewitz's tome, quite a few similarities can be noticed. In fact, there is plenty of helpful advice that can be applied to the business world. Naturally, there are occasions when it is somewhat impossible to see how this thinking might relate to business, such as when von Clausewitz addresses the nature of war in mountains or swamps. Believe me, I did my best to find something, but in the end I couldn't and so I focused instead on those elements of his book that are relevant to commerce. To make it a little easier, I have structured this book into broad themes, which makes his advice simpler to understand and also to apply.

So, I hope you find this book interesting, useful – and less painful to read than the original! Who knows, after this, you might even want to read *On War* for yourself.

1 WAR AS AN ACT OF HUMAN INTERCOURSE

War: Is it an art? Is it a science? No, it's just part and parcel of man's social existence.

DEFINING IDEA...

Art is I; science is we.
~ CLAUDE BERNARD,
FRENCH PHYSIOLOGIST

In *On War*, Carl von Clausewitz spends an age debating whether war should be considered an art or a science. Sparing you his reasoning, I can tell you now that he saw it as neither. In fact, he believed that if anything, war was more like commerce. As he points out, both war and commerce involve the clash of interests, although one obviously results in lots of bloodshed, the other lots of paperwork. In simple terms, war is directed at an animate object that reacts and for this very reason the nature of both art and science is inappropriate when applied to war. However, he did recognise that a huge range of human factors might be associated with war, including emotions, morals and intellectual capabilities. All served to create a mix that could never be codified into a series of rules or developed into an art form.

A similar debate has raged for years with respect to management theory. First, we had scientific management, which entailed breaking tasks down into their individual parts, building repetitive work activities around them and then training staff to perform each role. The result? Increased productivity. Then there was a bit of a backlash with the Human Relations movement, which suggested it was all about people: if you showed interest in your workforce, they would be more productive. It worked, too. This was followed by the view that it was a mix of both. So, it was clear that as with war, trying to make work into an art form or a science was futile because it involved individuals who would react and behave in unpredictable ways.

One company that seems to have cracked it, though, is Semco. This Brazilian business has no official structure, no organisational chart, no business plan, no strategy, no budget, no fixed CEO, no standards, no HR function, no job descriptions and no career plans. Yet Semco is very successful; its turnover is currently in excess of $160m, with over 3,000 staff employed. With broad business interests and operations in highly competitive markets, Semco's success lies in the way that it has placed employees at the heart of its organisation. Staff are involved in hiring and firing; they decide when they come to work and how to organise themselves; they choose whether Semco takes over another company and they get to experience the whole organisation by working in each of its 12 departments during their first 12 months. As a result, they understand the business, recognise what others bring to it and become part of the overall fabric. What CEO Ricardo Semler has realised is that like war, work is ultimately an act of human intercourse which is unpredictable, cannot be made into a science and is certainly not an art. If you let your staff get on with it, it kind of works – it's as simple as that.

HERE'S AN IDEA FOR YOU...

Because people lie at the heart of any organisation, it's important to treat them with due respect. Ask those around you (secretaries, colleagues and of course, your boss) what they think of your people skills – include direct reports, if you have them. Listen to what they say and use the feedback to improve your people-handling skills.

2 THE KNOWLEDGE REQUIRED IN WAR IS VERY SIMPLE

The basic knowledge required to execute war or manage a corporation might be very simple, but it takes time, intellect and a desire to learn in order to master it.

DEFINING IDEA...

True knowledge exists in knowing that you know nothing.
– SOCRATES, ANCIENT GREEK PHILOSOPHER

When von Clausewitz addresses the knowledge required in war he states that it is very simple – there really aren't that many skills to master – attack, defence, counterattack – and the number of associated factors – terrain, the weather, time of day, size of the army and so on – is also comparatively small. However, there is more to this than meets the eye; having the knowledge is one thing, applying it is completely different. Naturally the knowledge required in the lower ranks of the army is minimal, but von Clausewitz wasn't concerned about that. He was more concerned about the senior ranks, where knowledge had to be broad, although it need not be detailed. So, although the military leader had to know about the character, defects, strengths and weaknesses of the men he commanded, it was not necessary for him to be an acute observer of human behaviour.

By the same token, he had to know how long a column would take to march 50 miles in the driving rain, but he didn't need to know how to harness a battery horse. This breadth of skill could only be attained through a combination of personal reflection, study and thought. In other words, the commander had to master, manage and apply his knowledge expertly. In the final analysis, von Clausewitz believed no great commander was ever a man of limited intellect – so Richard Sharpe was unlikely ever to make General in real life, even though he might do so in fiction.

Like the higher and lower ranks of von Clausewitz's day, the knowledge required across a business varies. As expected, the knowledge required at the lowest levels in an organisation is usually quite limited. However, at the highest levels there must be people with a broad grasp of the business as a whole. And like the commander, they are not expected to understand the minutiae of marketing, but they do need to know how marketing can be used as a strategic tool. The same is true of sales, information technology, finance and so on. To be successful, senior staff must apply the same combination of reflection, study and thought as von Clausewitz's commanders. With today's levels of complexity and constant change, the breadth of knowledge we now have to master is significant, so it should come as no surprise that lifelong learning is of real interest to many corporations. The ability to learn is no longer something to be discarded when we finish school; it should be a lifelong skill. It is a shame that so many people, including many in senior positions, believe that learning is for cissies. Always remember, the wise man learns when he can; the fool learns when he has to.

HERE'S AN IDEA FOR YOU...

Do you understand the importance of lifelong learning to your career? Are you aware of what learning opportunities are available to you? Speak to HR to find out what they offer and find out what you can do to make learning central to your career. Once you understand, set yourself some learning objectives – and stick to them.

3 THEORY SHOULD BE STUDY, NOT DOCTRINE

Although war and indeed business can be learned from a book, practice is needed to master it.

DEFINING IDEA...

In theory, there is no difference between theory and practice. But, in practice, there is.

– YOGI BERRA, BASEBALL PLAYER

Von Clausewitz understood the nature of theory and practice in war; both were important, but of the two he was clear that theory should never be allowed to become military doctrine – if you like, a manual for war. Observing and analysing aspects of war to establish theory is in itself invaluable because this captures key components and sets out the critical aspects that really matter. The real job of theory in von Clausewitz's mind was twofold. First, it acts as a guide to anyone wishing to learn about war as it provides a rounded view of what it is all about and helps avoid the pitfalls and mistakes of others. Second, it exists so that no one new to war has to waste time trying to figure it all out. In the end, theory is designed to guide in self-education, not accompany to the battlefield. Just imagine Napoleon and Wellington holding a manual as they direct their troops at Waterloo – this would certainly not have instilled much confidence.

Accepting that theory has its place in the world of war, it is fair to say that it also sits well in business. Although there have been a few attempts to define commerce by the likes of Adam Smith (he of the invisible hand fame), key to developing a general theory for business was the launch of the world's first MBA programme, by Tuck Business School in the USA, in the early part of the twentieth century. Today, some 7,000 institutions offer MBA programmes to millions of budding (and existing) business executives, all hoping the theory of business will turn them into excellent businessmen and women. Defining the basic tenets of such concepts as marketing and human resources is of course a good thing and, like the theory of war, it can accelerate a novice's knowledge and help them get to grips with the nature of commerce. However, take heed of von Clausewitz's advice: just because you have an MBA under your belt, this does not, alas, make you the next Jack Welch or Richard Branson (both of whom do not have MBAs, by the way). Sure, it might make you smarter and allow you to spout some of the gobbledygook taught on such programmes, but it's no substitute for practical experience. Indeed, some pundits believe it was executives armed with MBAs who led us into the Credit Crunch and Great Recession of 2007–9. And if only to demonstrate the stupidity of relying on a theory of business, the Chinese now offer the Early MBA programme for three- to six-year-olds. Described as 'enrichment education for tomorrow's leaders', the course teaches mathematics, economics, astronomy and team building. Valuable? No. Insane? Absolutely.

HERE'S AN IDEA FOR YOU...

Problems need to be fully explored to allow you to bring all your experience and knowledge to bear on them. When problem solving, find a room with a whiteboard and give your brain more time to be creative; the results should speak for themselves.

4 ON HISTORICAL EXAMPLES

Henry Ford may have dismissed history as bunk, but I prefer Isaac Newton's quote on the shoulders of giants. After all, why learn the hard way when someone else has already done it for you?

DEFINING IDEA...

Those who cannot learn from history are doomed to repeat it.

~ GEORGE SANTAYANA, PHILOSOPHER, ESSAYIST, POET AND NOVELIST

Von Clausewitz was emphatic in his view that historical examples provide the best kind of proof in the study of war. His real concern, though, was the way in which theorists used such historical examples, which usually left the reader dissatisfied and irritated. This may explain why so many people hate history at school and now find it so dull; perhaps they just didn't have the right teacher or failed to read any of the great books out there. To put the reader straight, von Clausewitz lays out the proper and improper use of examples. He cites four key uses of historical examples. First, they may be used as an explanation of an idea; second, they serve to show the application of an idea; third, they can prove the possibility of a particular phenomenon or effect, and finally, they may be used to develop doctrine. Powerful stuff indeed and incredibly helpful, but he goes on to warn of the dangers too, such as only using those examples supporting a particular opinion.

If you're anything like me, you may have the odd medical every now and then. Worthwhile though they are, I'm always taken to task by my doctor because my cholesterol is slightly high. Always one to check things out, I began to investigate the nature of fat intake, cholesterol and heart disease.

And do you know what I found? Well, the received wisdom may in fact be bunk. According to medical researchers who have reviewed every single study in this area (in true von Clausewitzian style), the true enemy of the piece is carbohydrates, not fat. It transpires that many in the medical profession have only been using the research that supports their hypothesis that fat is bad for you and carbs are good (very naughty). And it seems they have misused the invaluable elements that can be gained from historical analysis. I wouldn't mind so much but I've been force-fed margarine for the last couple of years and it is, quite frankly, disgusting!

Although the business world is not quite the same as the medical profession, it is interesting to note many of the companies now beginning to dominate the world of industry and commerce are from the BRIC (Brazil, Russia, India and China) economies. They may be new but they have learned from their Western counterparts. Based so long in the USA and Europe, sector leaders are superseded by companies such as Tata Consultancy Services (technology), SAB Miller (brewing), Embraer (aircraft manufacture), América Móvil (telecoms), CNOOC (oil and gas) and Sadia (food and drink). Ultimately, history is an invaluable tool, to be ignored at your peril.

HERE'S AN IDEA FOR YOU...

The next time you have a report to write, find out what other companies have done first. Use this information to prepare a more comprehensive analysis and balanced report. Don't forget to consider organisations outside your own business sector too, as this gives you new and often invaluable insights.

5 WAR IS NEVER AN ISOLATED ACT

Although we like to believe that we can operate as an island, the truth is we are part of a wider system that controls us more than we could ever know.

DEFINING IDEA...

Great men are rarely isolated mountain peaks; they are the summits of ranges.

~ THOMAS HIGGINSON, US MINISTER, AUTHOR, ABOLITIONIST AND SOLDIER

In many ways von Clausewitz was ahead of his time, but there was one area in particular where he was light years ahead: systems thinking. Although systems theory as we know it today had yet to be defined or articulated, von Clausewitz understood war was not an isolated act. In his view, opponents in war could not regard each other as abstract entities; they were part of a wider system that included individual behaviour as well as politics. As a result, it was a relatively straightforward process to understand and model the motives of a potential enemy; all you had to do was observe. And because war was part of a larger 'system', it rarely broke out spontaneously nor could it spread instantaneously.

A perfect example of this is the run-up to World War I, in which a series of interlocking pacts and agreements such as the Entente Cordiale between Great Britain and France created conditions for global conflict. All that was needed was the spark – conveniently provided by Gavrilo Princip when he shot Archduke Franz Ferdinand on 28 June 1914. And because of the interconnected nature of the pacts, no one could have stopped the war, had they wanted to.

The concept of systems theory within an organisational setting didn't gain much traction until after the emergence of information technology (IT). IT provided the glue that connected not only the different functions within a business but individual companies, too. For example, our global finance system would not exist without the sophisticated trading platforms that tie investment and retail banks, central banks and trading floors across the world into a seamless whole. Wal-Mart too would not be able to hold down its prices in the way that it does without a global supply chain management system that tracks absolutely everything. Indeed, every business, even small ones, depend on IT and when you roll this up to the country or continental level, it is safe to say few businesses could be considered isolated. Each and every one is connected to all others, directly through trading relationships or indirectly via market forces and competition. Whether we like it or not, we are all part of a system and it's a good idea to understand how we are impacted by it; also how we can influence it. To do so requires a basic understanding of systems dynamics and systems thinking in which it is possible to model the various components and the interactions between them. Once you get the hang of it, systems thinking lets you model feedback loops and gain an understanding of how your business interacts with the wider markets in which it operates. It's great stuff!

HERE'S AN IDEA FOR YOU...

How do your decisions impact on others? Sometimes we don't know and this leads to unintended consequences and surprises. When making a decision, see how it affects other parts of the business and determine if the results are what you expect. If not, consider how you might change the decision to have a more effective outcome.

6 THE EFFECT OF THE POLITICAL AIM ON THE MILITARY OBJECTIVE

Governments have an awful habit of getting in the way of things, especially in times of war, but also in commerce.

DEFINING IDEA...

Business is business; it's not politics.

~ JACK MA, CHINESE INTERNET PIONEER

The medieval period was characterised by pacts, counterpacts and more counterpacts. Political scheming was the order of the day and it was difficult to keep track of the number of times political rivals would patch up old quarrels in order to gang up on their latest enemy only to break them again. Just ask the army – they were forced to keep popping over to the continent to press home the rights and demands of their monarchs. Even when one monarch offered the use of their army to another this was usually half-hearted and in any case the army was always controlled by the home nation, so there was little real control at all. For example, when the Scots teamed up with the Lancastrians during the latter stages of the Wars of the Roses (1461), they were more interested in pillaging than fighting and once they had satisfied their desire for cash, women and goods, they hot-footed it back to Scotland. Of course armies fight on behalf of their political masters and, as von Clausewitz quite rightly points out, war is nothing more than the continuation of politics by other means. So, war and politics go hand in hand.

Sometimes it seems that politics is as much of a pain in commerce as it is in war. I am not of course referring to the collusion between government officials and businessmen that happens a lot more than we like to imagine, but rather the way in which government policies can upset the status quo. Politicians have a tendency to interfere with established businesses through the introduction of new legislation or breaking up monopolies. In the main this is a good thing as it serves to protect the consumer and gives them greater choice. But if you happen to be running a major business, the costs associated with responding to the latest policy can be significant. I remember being involved in the introduction of domestic competition into the UK gas market back in the late 90s. The idea behind this was to break the monopoly that British Gas had over the supply of gas to the UK population. Irrespective of whether it has been good or bad for the market, it was an extremely costly exercise and highly disruptive too.

Not only did British Gas and Transco have to spend millions changing their processes, IT systems and organisational structures, but so too did their competitors. Although governments can do good things, such as forcing businesses to comply with health and safety legislation, they sometimes get carried away. For example, the current level of red tape caused by government policies is stifling small businesses and entrepreneurs, the very thing we need right now to generate growth. For once, it would be great if governments stopped interfering!

HERE'S AN IDEA FOR YOU...

Politics are part and parcel of any business and understanding the political environment is a key skill for any executive. Learn to be a wise owl so you both understand the necessity of politics and use it expertly. The best way is to observe how politics is applied by those in power.

7 THE CHARACTER OF CONTEMPORARY WARFARE

Keeping your strategies fresh means keeping a weather eye on how the world around you is changing.

DEFINING IDEA...

The art of life is a constant readjustment to our surroundings.

~ KAKUZO OKAKAURA, JAPANESE SCHOLAR

Von Clausewitz was crystal clear in his belief that changes in the way in which wars were fought heavily influenced strategic and tactical planning. In his view, every commander should pay particular attention to the character of contemporary warfare as part of the planning process and to prove the point he provided a few examples. He demonstrated how Bonaparte's audacity and luck blew away the accepted practices of war in the early nineteenth century and proved that it was possible to rapidly switch from defence to offence by citing how the Russians were able to drive Napoleon out of their country in 1812 (something they repeated in 1943 with the Germans). He believed that the best commanders always took the trouble to understand and adapt; so has GE.

GE has been in business since 1879 and is a very different company now to what it was then. The primary reason for long-term success has been its adaptability. GE's roots lie within the electricity industry, which in the late nineteenth century was still in its infancy. Even then, Thomas Alva Edison understood the need to adapt and was willing to experiment and build on others' work, exploiting this for financial gain. As well as protecting his 1,000 plus patents, he dominated his chosen markets through a combination of equity ownership, licensing and partnerships. Maintaining the company's position in the 20s and 30s involved a mix of franchising, controlling retail prices and relationship selling, although it was the application of the benign cycle strategy that allowed GE to maintain market dominance. By building and marketing an increasing number of electrical products greater demand for electricity was stimulated, which in turn forced the utility industry to upgrade their systems, which GE would supply. This allowed the company to remain profitable throughout the Depression and dominate the emerging radio and broadcasting industries.

In the 40s, when GE became heavily involved with the US war effort, focus shifted away from consumers and onto the military. The most significant dividend was diversification, which ensured the company was well positioned for the consumer boom that followed the end of World War II. When Jack Welch took over in 1981 he addressed the sacred cows within GE. He believed that if success was to continue, each business must either grow and lead their chosen markets or be sold off. In the first two years of his tenure Welch sold off 71 product lines and completed 188 deals. He epitomised GE's adaptability, which he encapsulated within six rules, of which two were key: change before you have to and control your destiny or someone else will. Jeff Immelt, who succeeded Neutron Jack in 2001, has continued to adjust GE to the changing economic and commercial environment, so it's fair to say the ability to adapt is in GE's corporate DNA.

HERE'S AN IDEA FOR YOU...

Change is part and parcel of the modern corporation and while some us embrace change, others don't. Are you open to change? If so, consider how you might help others to change when they need to. And if you fear change, seek to understand what personal barriers you put up when faced with change and learn to be more open.

8 GENERAL SURVEY

Good generals always take the trouble to understand what they're getting into. So too should any business.

When I was sixteen, I wanted to be a land surveyor and so I studied the subject at university. After graduation I joined the Ministry of Defence (Military Survey), where I had the chance to work in the deserts of northern Kenya. One key thing that was drummed into me when I was a student is that you always work from the whole to the part. In other words, it's essential to understand the bigger picture before getting into the detail. The simple reason why you'd want to do this is to reduce the potential for error. Von Clausewitz recognised this and back in the early nineteenth century he called this the bigger picture 'general survey'. He was clear that before any combat could take place it was essential to assess the necessary conditions for military action to avoid any mistakes and steer clear of annihilation. From the military perspective this covered the numerical strength and organisation of the opposing forces, their state when not in action, maintenance and supply, plus their relationship to the country and terrain in which they were fighting.

Like military leaders, companies also undertake general surveys from time to time. They need to understand how they are performing in relation to competitors, the effectiveness of their internal structures and processes and how the markets in which they sell and deliver their products and services are changing. And in the same way that general survey in von Clausewitz's era was used to inform the strategic planning for an upcoming battle, today's general survey informs the strategies of major corporations. Most leading businesses employ consultancies to complete their 'survey work' because they tend to be better at seeing the bigger picture and challenging the thinking of both CEO and board.

One consultancy has always stood out from the crowd: McKinsey & Company. Founded in Chicago, in 1926 by James O. McKinsey, a professor at the University of Chicago who pioneered budgeting as a management tool, the company has become one of the most sought-after and highly respected strategic consultancies worldwide. Much of their success is down to their hiring practices, in which only the brightest and most able recruits are taken on. But it is also due to the company's ability to crunch huge amounts of data to develop insights into the businesses they consult with. Masters of the general survey for the corporate world, they are expert at hoovering up and disseminating knowledge and insights through their many publications, such as *McKinsey Quarterly*. Although frequently criticised over how difficult it is to implement their advice, McKinsey & Company continue to consult with 60% of the world's largest companies. And as I often tell my wife: I can make maps, but I can't use them.

HERE'S AN IDEA FOR YOU...

If you were to undertake a general survey of your company, what aspects would you consider? Who might you consult? Research your own organisation to find out more about it. This allows you to become more connected and demonstrates an interest in your company and its overall development.

9 RELATIONSHIP BETWEEN THE BRANCHES OF THE SERVICE

Armies, like organisations, tend to have the same branches. How they are used and their relative importance varies, though.

When it came to discussing the relationship between the branches of the army, von Clausewitz focused on the Infantry, Artillery and Cavalry – no planes, tanks or Predators back then, I'm afraid. Although all three were important, their actual deployment varied considerably and depended on the nature of the enemy, the availability of men and arms, and of course the relative strengths and weaknesses of individual branches. The Artillery packed plenty of firepower, but was immobile and vulnerable. If captured it could be used by the enemy. In contrast, the Cavalry were very mobile and could do a fantastic job in attack, but were generally ineffective when it came to defence, being the weakest branch. And finally, the Infantry could pack quite a bit of firepower. Excellent on defence and pretty good at attack, they were the strongest of all.

The composition of an army also varied. For example, if firepower was critical, greater emphasis would be placed on the Artillery whereas if mobility was more of a factor, the proportion of Cavalry would be higher. Summing up, von Clausewitz suggests the key questions to ask when determining the best combination of the three branches are how much Artillery can be deployed without it becoming a disadvantage and how little Cavalry can you get away with? To be truly effective, all three had to be present, though.

Similar rules apply to organisations. A typical business has a standard set of functions: HR, sales, marketing, IT, operations and so forth. There will be others addressing the specific needs of the industry sector, too. Like the three branches of the army, the relative importance of individual functions depends on a range of factors, such as the market in which they trade, the importance of technology and the current economic climate. For example, investment banks are principally sales focused, so the majority of their resources are geared towards the front office and everything else is secondary. This explains why so much power and testosterone resides with the traders, who can run roughshod over everyone else in the organisation. Companies like Microsoft are mainly focused on technology and how this can be exploited in their products. Although less critical, HR is geared to the recruitment of high-calibre staff. Airlines such as British Airways place greater emphasis on engineering because the safety of their passengers is of the highest importance. Let's face it, who'd want to travel on an airline that cares more about catering than engineering? As BA and their competitors adjust to the collapse in air travel following the Credit Crunch, they are cutting back on non-essential operational roles and cabin staff rather than engineering. Like the army in von Clausewitz's time, all branches are important, but some will always be more so than others.

HERE'S AN IDEA FOR YOU...

If you really want to find out how your business works, spend some time with a representative from each of the main functions (sales, finance, marketing, HR, etc.). Ask them what they do and how they interact with other parts of the company. This allows you to develop a more rounded view of how your organisation operates.

10 THE ORDER OF BATTLE

An army has to be well organised and adjust its order of battle to take into account new ways of killing the enemy. Similarly, a business must be well organised to survive and needs to exploit the latest means of killing off the competition.

DEFINING IDEA...

Every new change forces all the companies in an industry to adapt their strategies to that change.

~ BILL GATES, CO-FOUNDER OF MICROSOFT

War has always been synonymous with innovation, with millions of years spent dreaming up new and improved ways of killing each other. Indeed, it is well known that wars, especially world wars, lead to major advancements in the use of technology that might otherwise take years to achieve, if at all. Face it: we might never have landed on the moon, had it not been for World War II.

Von Clausewitz witnessed how the introduction of the firearm changed the way the army was organised for battle – it allowed the Infantry to be greatly expanded and cover a wider portion of the battlefield. However, this also meant that the Cavalry, so long an integral part of the fighting whole, had to be kept out of harm's way which made it much harder to manage the total fighting force. All this changed in the 1750s when military planners realised that instead of having to manage a whole army, they could split it up into a smaller number of corps with elements of every part of the army within them. As a result it was possible to introduce strategy into the fighting and rather than just one great big free-for-all in the middle of the battlefield, they could do all sorts of interesting things like pincer movements and deploy mobile units of irregular soldiers.

Organisations need an effective order of battle too: their divisional structures and business units. These are the organisational equivalent of the army corps, each focused on their part of the market. Like the army, they too need to adjust to changes in technology and market conditions. If they can't (in some cases won't), they'll find themselves on the losing side. And like those who thought the longbow could take on the musket, or a Cavalry unit could take on a Panzer division, some fail to see the change until it's too late. In 1992, this happened to IBM when it failed to recognise the significance of the personal computer and Microsoft's role in it. As they scoffed at the bunch of geeky college dropouts, they gave control of the operating system to Microsoft. Within a year they were haemorrhaging money and profits dropped by $800m.

Only after reducing costs by $9 billion, sacking 80,000 staff and re-engineering the business was the corner finally turned. IBM learned the importance of the order of battle the hard way. Now, as they seek to exploit the shift to green technologies, it's changing again. This time it won't be quite so painful. No doubt von Clausewitz would have been proud.

HERE'S AN IDEA FOR YOU…

Sometimes the way a business operates makes no sense, but there's normally a good reason why it is the way it is. Speak to your strategy managers to find out how the markets in which your company operates impact your business. This will help you to understand how you fit in and what is expected of you.

11 BASE OF OPERATIONS

Establishing and maintaining a powerful relationship between base and the field is essential, both in war and business. With this, you can literally rule the world.

DEFINING IDEA...

We are not a global business.
We are a collection of local businesses
with intense global coordination.
– PERCY BARNEVIK, SWEDISH GLOBAL EXECUTIVE

When an army commences operations it is dependent on its base for supply, orders and replenishment – these constitute the foundation for its existence and survival. Eventually, the sheer size and geographical location of the army makes it difficult to maintain an effective link between the base and the men in the field, however. This is where outposts, depots and other fortifications come into their own, which is of course why there are so many castles dotted around Europe – keeping unruly locals in check would have been impossible otherwise. Von Clausewitz was quick to point out that it was impractical to provide definitive advice on where to site such bases, or indeed how best to manage them. In his view, it was a case of dealing with each one on an individual basis taking into account a range of factors, including terrain, availability of resources and lines of communication. Tricky though this might be, it can be done – just look at how well the Romans managed to control most of the known world in AD 14.

The need for an effective and strong relationship between a business and its outlying operations is equally important. Although not focused on keeping unruly populations in check, it is necessary to keep errant managers and employees focused on what they should be doing. So many organisations expand into the far reaches of the world only to fail to exercise proper control.

The only time they seem to get hot and bothered and exert their authority is when revenues collapse and profits fall. By then of course it is way too late and the effort required to bring operations to heel can be expensive and time consuming. However, one organisation has cracked it: ABB.

A global leader in power and automation technologies, ABB operates in more than 100 countries through a network of 87 offices. Created out of the merger of ASEA of Sweden and Brown, Boveri & Cei of Switzerland, it has achieved an amazing degree of convergence and consistency across a wide range of countries and cultures. It has done so by preserving and promoting the local cultures of the companies it acquires but at the same time creates a global culture that ensures it does not fracture into national islands. So, although its factories are spread across the world, they all form part of global groups that share technology and best practice. Cross-border cooperation is also enhanced through the use of multicultural teams. Few of ABB's profit centres are viable as stand-alone entities: each depends on the other for ideas, information and resources. This is a company that truly understands the importance of a strong base of operations. Hopefully, others will follow their example.

HERE'S AN IDEA FOR YOU...

Consider how your organisation manages and controls its subsidiaries. Do you believe them to be effective, or does just too much fire fighting and internal politics go on? What needs to change to make them as slick as ABB?

12 LINES OF COMMUNICATION

If you really want to know what's going on, keep your lines of communication simple and direct.

DEFINING IDEA...

The ear of the leader must ring with the voices of the people.

~ WOODROW WILSON, US PRESIDENT

Today, the nature of communication in war is a complex, multimedia affair but in the mid eighteenth and early nineteenth centuries, it was much more basic. Back then, there were no telephones or videoconferencing facilities. The equivalent of the digital superhighway was the road system. Roads were not only used to provide the army with much-needed supplies, they were also critical for couriers – transporting the dead and wounded from the battlefield – and of course running away from the enemy when things got hairy. Von Clausewitz recognised that if the distance between the army and its source of information and supplies was too long or difficult to use, then the army as a whole would suffer. Given the lines of communication were so critical to the health of the army, every effort was made to keep them open, effective and as short as possible.

From a business perspective, the invention of the telephone by Alexander Graham Bell in 1876 irrevocably changed our lines of communication. Its invention launched an ongoing revolution. This has not only heralded the death of distance, allowing businesses to communicate with any part of the world, at any time of day, but also made them communication rich, allowing every part of the business to be an integral part of the lines of communication. And of all the technologies, email has had the most impact.

The unfortunate thing about this revolution is that we no longer communicate effectively and we have lost some of the simple axioms of von Clausewitz's time. Email is especially dangerous, even more so with the advent of the BlackBerry. No longer willing to communicate face-to-face, everyone seems happy to send an inordinate number of electronic messages, which in the main are ignored, pointless, inflammatory or misunderstood. Then there are the crazy people who, despite sitting next to a colleague, choose to communicate via email. Sure, the lines of communication are short, but are they effective? There's no doubt the art of communication has been lost and organisations no longer seem capable of making every effort to keep communication channels open, effective and as short as possible.

Fortunately, some of the more forward-looking corporations like Intel have introduced no-email days in which its employees must discuss the issues of the day face-to-face and reacquaint themselves with some of the subtleties of effective communication, like looking into the whites of the eyes of those they are talking to and being attuned to body language. They can also remember the importance of other aspects of human interaction, such as getting to the point quickly and working as a team. Who knows, if this is practised enough, we might even begin to recapture some of the essence of what effective communication meant in 1750.

HERE'S AN IDEA FOR YOU...

Are you someone who depends on BlackBerry and email to communicate? If so, try breaking the habit and communicate face-to-face at least one day a week. You may be surprised at the results and end up choosing face-to-face as your preferred communication style.

13 MAINTENANCE AND SUPPLY

Just as the armies in von Clausewitz's era needed effective supply lines to win their campaigns, today's global businesses must have efficient and effective supply chains to dominate their markets.

DEFINING IDEA...

Think globally, act locally, think tribally, act universally.

– JOHN NAISBITT, FUTUROLOGIST

Von Clausewitz was writing at a time when the nature of warfare was fundamentally changing. Following the Peace of Westphalia, signed in 1648 and which ended the Thirty Years War, warfare gradually became more connected and more of a continuous affair with armies typically engaged in fighting and manoeuvres for all but the winter months. Armies also became more professional and better trained. Von Clausewitz recognised that with larger armies being the norm, the importance of keeping them well supplied was becoming more operationally demanding. This combination of size and length of operations increased the importance of logistics and supply; without an effective approach even the most comprehensive of victories could soon be lost.

Love it or hate it, Wal-Mart is singularly the most successful retail organisation of all time. Whether you consider it to be a bully or a beacon, it sells some really good stuff – and very, very cheaply. One of the principal reasons why Wal-Mart continues to be so successful is its obsessive focus on developing and maintaining a highly efficient supply chain. Like von Clausewitz, Wal-Mart understands the problems arising from continuous operations and scale. As the world's largest retailer, it offers a vast range of products delivered to the stores through automated distribution centres and an inventory system that allows shipping times to be significantly reduced. Achieving this has been possible by cutting out intermediaries, working closely with suppliers and adopting the latest supply chain technologies.

Central to its success has been the willingness of Wal-Mart to embrace its suppliers, collocating them at their Bentonville headquarters (not that they were given much choice, of course). For example, Proctor & Gamble have 400 of their employees based there and have been joined by staff from Wal-Mart's other 500 suppliers. Here, they work together continuously to enhance the supply chain processes so that both Wal-Mart and their suppliers benefit. As part of this process, Wal-Mart also launched an initiative to overcome the inconsistent supply chain language used across its supplier base and developed, with Accenture's support, a Retail Supply Chain Certification Programme. The benefits of this are clear, especially to Wal-Mart, which has reduced time spent debating inventory policy definitions, forecasts and other technical details.

Since Wal-Mart was established in 1962, the nature of the retail sector has changed dramatically. Trade has globalised and the demand for products increased, both in number and variety. Wal-Mart understood that if it was going to succeed, it had to get to grips with how best to deal with these dual pressures. Like von Clausewitz, Wal-Mart concluded it was all about supply – that, and selling goods for incredibly low prices. I for one always make a beeline for Wal-Mart when I'm in the US.

HERE'S AN IDEA FOR YOU...

Next time you sit down with a supplier consider discussing how you can work together more closely. Rather than piling on the pressure, find ways to enhance the relationship for your mutual benefit. If you understand some of the issues they face, you can work together to resolve them and the outcome will be better for everyone.

14 METHOD AND ROUTINE

Armies and organisations are just the same: both need routine to run like well-oiled machines.

Let's face it, most of us hate routine: doing the same thing over and over can be a real drag. It's soul-destroying and does little for motivation, especially if you work in accounts. But just imagine if there was no routine at all. Work would be a total disaster; there would be no consistency and it's unlikely anything would get done. Bet your bottom dollar it wouldn't be long before everyone was crying out for some kind of routine. Von Clausewitz understood the importance of method and routine to an army and ultimately to the conduct of war. Both provided the necessary foundation for solid discipline and the unthinking actions required in the heat of battle. Indeed, he recognised that the constant practice that came with routine led to brisk, precise and reliable leadership, which reduced natural friction and eased the working of the army machine. He also points out that routines represent a general way of executing tasks: they arise and represent the dominance of principles and rules carried through to actual application. So although it might appear dull that squaddies march around the parade ground all day, or spend hours spit-polishing their boots and stripping down weapons, this serves the essential purpose of developing solid discipline.

Fortunately, those of us not in the army don't have to spend hours polishing our shoes or marching round a parade ground. However, we still need routine. Without it, we'll be unable to deliver consistent products and services to our customers. And the way we impose routine is through well-defined standardised processes. In the past, achieving consistent and effective processes has proved impossible and even when the business process re-engineering zealots steamrollered their way through the corporations of the 90s, the process nirvana they hoped to impose was a total disaster. Even today many organisations wouldn't know a standardised process if it punched them in the face. And yes, even in accounting, probably the most simple of business disciplines to standardise.

Fortunately, over the recent past a huge amount of effort has gone into developing processes that can literally be picked off the shelf and applied to any business context. For example, Massachusetts Institute of Technology (MIT) has created an online process handbook containing 5,000-plus processes and activities and the American Productivity and Quality Center (APQC) has developed a process classification framework describing every process you might expect to find in a typical organisation. So there's really no excuse for having multiple versions of the same process anymore; it's bad for business and very bad for your soul. Just imagine the exciting work you could be doing instead of chasing the errors caused by inconsistent processes. Routine, bring it on!

HERE'S AN IDEA FOR YOU...

Given we all use processes in our day-to-day work, it's a good idea to review the ones you use. Are they well defined, well documented and simple to use? Or is there room for improvement? If so, redesign them to be more efficient.

15 TERRAIN

Terrain and markets might seem quite different: after all, one is more critical to the military commander and the other to a business leader, but their detailed understanding is essential to success.

DEFINING IDEA...

The aim of marketing is to know and understand the customer so well the product or service fits him and sells itself.

~ PETER DRUCKER, MANAGEMENT GURU

There are many factors that a military commander must consider before attacking an enemy. The relative strength of the opposing army is one, supply another, but one of the most important considerations is terrain. Because the geography of the battlefield and its surrounding area can have a decisive influence on the outcome of an engagement, commanders worth their salt take this into consideration when planning a campaign. Many of the famous battles fought throughout history have used terrain to good effect: Thermopylae in 480 BC, Agincourt in 1415 and Waterloo in 1815, for example. From von Clausewitz's perspective, terrain can affect military operations in three ways: it creates an obstacle to the approach, acts as a barrier to visibility and provides protection from fire. Critical stuff indeed and even in today's high-tech military, terrain remains an essential element of military doctrine.

Broaden the notion of what terrain might mean and markets could be the organisational equivalent. Markets are the lifeblood of any organisation selling products and services and because of this, companies employ lots of clever marketing people who will, among many other tasks, undertake detailed research and hold customer focus groups. Market knowledge is vital and the time when it matters most is when a new product is launched.

The story of Lexus,* Toyota's luxury brand, perfectly illustrates how a detailed understanding of the market pays off. In the early 80s Toyota wanted to build a car that was better than anything the luxury car market could offer. Achieving this took six years and involved thousands of engineers, hundreds of prototypes and almost 2m test miles. Absolutely everything was placed under the microscope: fuel efficiency, speed, weight, performance, handling, noise and so on. Perfection meant ensuring everything was perfect and so they assembled the dream team, figured out their targets (the Mercedes S Class and the BMW 7 Series) and then they got under the skin of the customer. Really getting to know the market meant understanding the luxury lifestyle, so they packed the team off to cities like New York, San Francisco and Chicago, where they shopped in expensive malls, ate in high-end restaurants, enjoyed membership at exclusive country clubs and indulged in the whole luxury experience. Their observations were enhanced by input from anthropologists, psychologists and focus groups. Although undoubtedly a lot of fun, this was vital research because Toyota found out what the rich wanted from a car. And it really paid off: when the LS400 was launched in 1989, not only did it surprise the car market, it also came top in every category that mattered. Toyota had mastered the art of understanding terrain and beat the best the luxury car market had to offer. Job done!

*May, M. (2007), *The Elegant Solution: Toyota's formula for mastering innovation.* New York: Free Press, pp 42–9.

HERE'S AN IDEA FOR YOU...

How well does your company understand its markets? What action does it take to ensure this? Review some of your marketing literature and see if you can understand the market the product or service is selling into. Are you convinced? What is missing?

16 FORTRESSES

Fortresses can be considered barriers to entry. In the past these were made of stone; today, however, they could be a number of things.

DEFINING IDEA...

In business, the competition will bite you if you keep running. If you stand still, they will swallow you.

~ VICTOR KIAM, US BUSINESSMAN

Whenever a lord fell out with the king during medieval times he could retreat behind the walls of his castle. Even kings had to do this from time to time when their subjects became overly aggressive and demanding. Fortunately, they usually had lots of men at arms to hack errant subjects to death. Although primarily designed for defence, the strategic qualities of fortresses were not lost on marauding armies and often formed part of an invasion plan. In fact, sometimes armies were only concerned with capturing the castles as these gave them control over huge swathes of the country in which they were fighting. However, von Clausewitz was principally concerned with defence and lists their principal qualities which include acting as depots for armaments and supplies, providing protection to local populations, forming barriers to an invading army and acting as focal points for insurrections. From his perspective, fortresses were the primary barrier to entry of his time.

Although many corporate headquarters resemble fortresses, few have standing armies with which to defend them. However, companies are concerned about maintaining their market share, locking in customers and keeping the competition at bay. Otherwise they wouldn't have much of a business and it's unlikely they would survive too long. Most important is the desire to keep new entrants away from their markets and they do this by creating barriers to entry – the latter-day equivalent of a fortress, if you like. Barriers to entry are the unique characteristics that define an industry and also prevent other companies from entering. Michael Porter, one of the great business gurus of the twentieth century, developed the now-famous Five Forces model, which allows you to assess the key influences on an industry. The five forces were: supplier power, threat of substitutes, buyer power, degree of rivalry and of course, barriers to entry. This model has become an indispensible tool in strategic planning.

When it came to barriers to entry, Porter identified plenty, but three are particularly effective. First, government policy and its associated legislation can be a powerful barrier to entry even though it is often focused on maintaining a level playing field. For example, draconian regulation prevents new businesses from entering the utility sector. The second is through proprietary knowledge and patents. Having registered a patent, it is possible to keep rivals at bay; should they step onto your turf, you can sue them – which usually does the trick. And third, if the industry requires specialist equipment that may be very expensive to procure, this usually acts as a significant barrier to entry. That's why you don't see many start-up oil businesses. Today's barrier to entry may not be made of stone, but it can be highly effective in keeping unwanted competition out of your markets.

HERE'S AN IDEA FOR YOU...

Identify the barriers to entry that allow your company to keep new entrants out of your markets. When reviewing these, consider how effective they are and what others might be available to you, such as use of technology, pricing and customer relationship management.

17 BILLETS

Accommodation for the foot soldier on campaign and the wage slave in the office has a major impact on their effectiveness so it's a good idea to take this seriously.

DEFINING IDEA...

Every time I bestow a vacant office I make a hundred discontented persons and one ingrate.
~ LOUIS XIV, FRENCH KING

For a long time the life of the soldier on campaign was pretty grim. Not only did they march in all weathers, but they also had to find what little shelter they could at night, which in the main meant very little. However, as armies became larger, more sophisticated and better equipped, they could at least spend the night under canvass. But even this level of luxury could not prevent illness, which did little for the morale of the men. Von Clausewitz was sympathetic to their plight and felt that buildings rather than tents were always a better option. The location and shape of the billets was of particular concern to him, as determining the best place to site them required careful consideration. For example, if the commander had to muster his troops quickly, he would have to select buildings in close proximity. His favoured configuration was an oblong close to being a square or circle – this catered for most requirements.

Just as troops must be properly billeted to keep them as effective as possible, employees need office space that ensures their productivity is maximised. Like many people, I have worked in all kinds of buildings over the years – ones without windows, ones with no private office space and others where there were private offices and nothing else. Some have been great to work in, others sucked. But it's quite amazing how the space in which you work each day affects a whole range of things, including your ability to do your job, your attitude to your employer, how many hours you put in and your general level of job satisfaction. For example, in one company I had to endure an ex-army colonel who would bellow across the open-plan office, disturbing in the region of two hundred people in the process. Not one to speak quietly, he would even shout when he made presentations to small groups. You always knew when he was in; he was a complete nightmare and not particularly good for one's concentration. Everyone was delighted when he left – their ears stopped bleeding too.

Amusing though this might be, it's shocking that so many companies fail to understand the significance of the space where their employees work and how critical this is. The whole move to open-plan offices might have saved cash, but the amount lost due to reductions in productivity has been far greater. Fortunately, there have been plenty of studies highlighting the crucial link between office space, productivity and employee commitment. In the end a well-thought out office space is like a good billet: it does wonders for morale.

HERE'S AN IDEA FOR YOU...

Take a good look around your office space. Is it designed to promote productivity and commitment, or is it badly conceived? What simple changes could you instigate to improve it? If you are responsible for a team, ask them to contribute to the changes. If they look good, you'll look good too.

18 MORAL FACTORS

Morality is the cornerstone of success in war. So if it can be achieved under such difficult conditions, why is it so hard for business leaders and politicians to act morally?

DEFINING IDEA...

To know what is right and not to do it is the worst cowardice.

– CONFUCIUS, CHINESE PHILOSOPHER

Von Clausewitz was unequivocal in his belief that morals constituted the spirit that permeated war. And although they could not be classified or counted, they could no more be omitted from the theory of the art of war than any of the other components. Morals, he stated, ran through his entire treatise as did the physical side of war, but the former was more important. In fact, von Clausewitz likened the physical side of war to little more than a wooden hilt and the moral side to the finely honed blade within it. Although he dismissed the idea of attempting to list or indeed measure morals, he took the trouble to identify the principal moral elements: the skill of the commander, the experience and courage of the troops and their patriotic spirit. None of these, or the need for morality could be underestimated. In his mind, all were equally important.

Of course, morals transcend war and are fundamental to the effective functioning of any society or business, large or small. Without them everything would break down and it would be a free-for-all – which sounds fun for about five minutes, after which you must arm yourself. Of course, no one said that leading a corporation or indeed a country was ever easy, but those who want power and seek out such positions must understand that everyone else expects them to behave in a way commensurate with their high office.

They are looked up to and those who are led assume, rightly or wrongly, that those in power are better than they are in every respect. A leader with a solid moral compass can do great things, but one who lacks true morality destroys the trust that matters so much and holds everything together. Unfortunately, over the last decade we have seen too many companies with corrupt leaders – WorldCom, Enron and Parmalat; too many conmen and Ponzi schemers such as Bernie Madoff who take people for a ride and corrupt leaders such as Robert Mugabe, who enrich themselves while their countrymen starve to death.

But the unscrupulous, self-serving behaviour of politicians, the very people who define the moral compass for the rest of the country, topped it all in 2009. Far from being whiter than white, it transpired that they had behaved like pigs at a trough, filling their boots with taxpayers' money to fund their property empires, tend their gardens and pay for the occasional Mars Bar. Having been rumbled, they blamed the system instead of fessing up to their crimes. I am pretty certain von Clausewitz would have a lot to say about that. Who knows, he might even decide to run them through with his finely honed blade.

HERE'S AN IDEA FOR YOU...

Write down what you consider to be the ten key moral traits you expect to see in a business leader. Use these to measure the managers in your company. Do they measure up? And how about you? What changes might you make to set a good example?

19 ON MILITARY GENIUS

There's a simple reason why genius is limited to all but a few: war, business and, in fact, life in general would be a nightmare if there were too many.

DEFINING IDEA...

Genius does what it must,
and Talent does what it can.
– OWEN MEREDITH, EARL OF LYTTON

When von Clausewitz turned his attention to the nature of military genius he started by pointing out that any complex activity, if it is to be carried out with any degree of skill, requires the appropriate gifts of intellect and temperament (in today's HR language, we would call this talent). And if these are outstanding and reveal themselves in exceptional achievements, then the person possessing them could rightly be called a genius. He recognised, of course, that genius varied considerably and was arguably more prevalent in societies considered more civilised and advanced. Even so, true genius was a rare commodity. Thank heavens, therefore, that the execution of war does not require an army's rank and file to be full of geniuses. If it did, we would be in real trouble. In the final analysis, von Clausewitz believed the type of person most likely to display the qualities of military genius would possess an enquiring rather than creative mind, a comprehensive rather than specialised approach and a calm, rather than an excitable head. All useful stuff, but there was an essential subtext to his analysis and that was context. This had a massive bearing on whether or not someone might be perceived to be a genius.

What about genius in the workplace? There's no doubt that there are plenty of clever and talented people in the world of commerce and certain professions such as law attract some of the sharpest minds. But such people, no matter how clever they might be, can only really be considered talented. True genius is as rare now as it has ever been and perhaps business is not the place to find it. However, in the same way as the young Mozart stood head and shoulders above his peers, there are businesspersons who stand out from their peer group. Some are clearly very good, like Richard Branson or Lakshmi Mittal, and others are central to their companies, such as Steve Jobs of Apple. But real genius? I believe that business genius is about being more than competent at managing a company, it's taking a commanding role, seeing what's next, combining the three qualities of military genius with context. For me the one businessman who could be considered a genius is Jack Welch. Not only was he one of the best leaders GE had ever had, but he also developed much of the management thinking that we now take for granted. More than just business or creative talent, this took real genius.

And for those of you who wish they were geniuses, just remember that Mozart died a pauper and Napoleon was poisoned while in exile on the island of St Helena. Genius, who needs it?

HERE'S AN IDEA FOR YOU...

Talent is vital to any business and being able to nurture and develop those with exceptional abilities is essential to a high-performing company. How does your organisation identify and nurture its talent? HR should know this and be able to advise you. That way, if a member of your team shows outstanding flair, you'll know what to do.

20 THE THIRST FOR FAME AND HONOUR

Ego is something that can be of huge benefit at a time of war, but in business big egos often mean big problems.

DEFINING IDEA...

The sin of Hubris is inevitably and inexorably followed by Nemesis.

~ ROBERT TOWNSEND, FORMER AVIS CEO

These days, we live in a world obsessed with celebrity, where everyone seems to want their fifteen minutes of fame. One of the principal drivers of this obsession is ego and it's important to understand that we all have one. Most of the time our egos are held in check, but there are some people whose ego is bigger than they are, and that's when things get interesting. Von Clausewitz understood that the longing for honour and renown was a powerful motivator in a military commander. Although other emotions such as patriotism, idealism, vengeance and enthusiasm might be more common and more venerated, alone they are insufficient to give the commander the ambition to strive higher than the rest, which he must do if he is to distinguish himself. Von Clausewitz leaves the subject with the following poser: 'We may well ask whether history has ever known a great general who was not ambitious; whether, indeed, such a figure is conceivable.'

Although he acknowledged that the downside of ego could be highly damaging, von Clausewitz was highly dismissive of the German language, which tarnishes ambition and ego with two ignoble phrases 'greed for honour' (Ehrgeiz) and 'hankering after glory' (Rhumsucht). He had a point: the nature of conflict demands a big ego. Without it, it would be difficult to win any major engagement. Napoleon, Hitler and Macarthur were all driven by their egos and although each of them did some pretty amazing things, ultimately their egos got the better of them. That's what happens and it's a rare individual with a big ego who has not suffered because of it. Still, no one likes a fathead, do they?

Businesses are like armies: they require strong commanders to lead them. And business leaders are no different from the egocentric military commander who craves honour and renown. Ego is a necessary component of business success and so long as the ego is not massive, the results can be fantastic. Indeed, some leaders are idolised by their staff and lionised by the press – for good reason. They do great things and drive their businesses to new heights. However, ego is a double-edged sword. Leaders with big egos are self-obsessed and when this goes unchecked (for example, by the board, non-executives or institutional shareholders), they can do immense harm to a company and even, in extreme cases, cause it to fail. Some business leaders are so narcissistic that they end up believing that they are the company and everything else is subordinate to them. This is when you see executives such as Bernard Ebbers, Kenneth Lay and Dennis Kozlowski treating their companies as convenient piggybanks, having lost sight of the fact that they are meant to be running it on behalf of the shareholders. Fortunately, erstwhile bodies such as the SEC and the FED keep such crazy people in check.

HERE'S AN IDEA FOR YOU...

So, what's your boss like? How about the CEO? Do they have massive egos? Consider what the upsides and downsides might be and identify where ego can be positive for the business and where it might be damaging.

21 ON DANGER

War is, of course, highly dangerous and usually involves the loss of life. Work doesn't really involve much danger, but it can still be highly risky.

DEFINING IDEA...

Danger is the spur of all great minds.

~ GEORGE CHAPMAN, ENGLISH POET

Anyone who has watched the opening sequence of *Saving Private Ryan* will be well aware that war involves plenty of danger; of that we can be certain. But when discussing the nature of danger in war, von Clausewitz points out that anyone who has not experienced danger first-hand appears to be more attracted than alarmed by it. This kind of makes sense and explains why many of us love roller coasters so much – they provide that near-death experience without actually dying. Von Clausewitz doesn't spend too much time dwelling on danger, apart from providing a blow-by-blow account for the novice and stating that when faced with danger, ordinary qualities are not enough. He concludes with a wonderful remark: Without an accurate conception of danger, we cannot understand war.

Naturally work does not involve the levels of danger we associate with war, but it can involve a lot of risk. And we could take von Clausewitz's final word on danger and reword it for businesses thus: Without an accurate conception of risk, we cannot understand business. Taking risks is the lifeblood of any corporation and without some risk there can be no opportunity, or indeed reward. But in the same way that a novice warrior is drawn to war with a sense of excitement and fascination, certain individuals and indeed companies are drawn towards excessive risk-taking without fully comprehending the consequences (or perhaps ignoring them). We have recently been reminded of this by the financial turbulence and resulting recession caused by investment banks such as Lehman Brothers and insurance companies like AIG. By taking what many now consider unnecessary risks with other people's money they almost brought down the entire global finance system. This of course is not the first time – I saw it first-hand when the clever chaps at Long Term Capital Management almost succeeded back in 1998. Who knows, perhaps some day someone will do so.

Of course what usually happens after a collapse as significant as the one witnessed in 2007 and 2008 is a massive shift to risk aversion. Now don't get me wrong, those who screwed up so royally must be held to account and some additional regulation is no doubt required to protect the broader economy, but we should guard against taking it too far. If that happens, organisations will seize up, no one will be prepared to take a risk and we'll all end up working for the government. Risk is as essential to business as danger is to war. A good risk management framework resembles a great roller-coaster ride: it takes you to the end of your seat, but brings you back safely and in one piece. So go on, take a bit of risk, but manage it carefully.

HERE'S AN IDEA FOR YOU...
Ask to review the risk management processes for your organisation. Consider whether they are too onerous and will stifle risk taking, or perhaps too loose and encourage reckless behaviour. Maybe they're about right and will allow your business to thrive. How can you apply them to your job?

22 BOLDNESS

When it came to prosecuting a war, in von Clausewitz's view there was nothing better than boldness. In his view, anyone could be bold, but boldness governed by superior intellect, now that was the mark of a hero.

DEFINING IDEA...

Nobody ever defended anything successfully; there is only attack and attack and attack some more.
~ GENERAL GEORGE S. PATTON

In Book Three von Clausewitz focuses on strategy in general but soon narrows in on what he considers to be the key tenets, of which boldness is one. He states that whenever boldness encounters timidity, it is likely to be the winner because timidity in itself implies a loss of equilibrium. He is also very clear that although boldness is an essential quality in the rank and file of the army, it is important to temper this with a reflective mind the higher up the chain of command you go. In other words, being a bull in a china shop is okay when you are a private, but not much use for a general. To be successful at this level you must think before you act. And although Red Bull can give you wings these days, back in von Clausewitz's time, it was boldness tempered with intellect that did the trick. And with their wings, von Clausewitz's heroes could do wonderful things.

Michael O'Leary is the larger-than-life CEO of Ryanair and well known for his public outbursts, amusing antics and for charging his customers for absolutely everything – even, it has been suggested, for using the toilet on his planes. However, when he took over the reins of Ryanair, the company had accumulated £20 m in debt while attempting to take on the might of established airlines, British Airways and Aer Lingus. O'Leary recognised that the initial strategy of undercutting Ryanair's rivals by 50% would never be successful because their competitors had deeper cash reserves and could easily force them out of business. He understood that the discounting had to be much deeper and increased this to 90%. At this level it would be impossible for their competitors to respond without significantly impacting their profits. However, O'Leary knew that cheap fares alone would not make the airline successful or drive profitable growth, so he embarked on fundamentally re-engineering the business model to support his vision of a profitable low-fare airline. The result of his transformation speaks for itself. By 1995 Ryanair overtook Aer Lingus and British Airways to become the largest passenger airline on the Dublin to London route; in 2002 the company became Europe's number one airline for customer service and the world's largest international airline in terms of numbers in 2007.

The success of O'Leary is classic von Clausewitz – boldness tempered with intellect. He understood what needed to be done and didn't shy away from the necessities of corporate battle (after all, that is what it is) and continues to drive innovation into the airline business, forcing rivals to respond – even if that does mean charging customers to go to the loo.

HERE'S AN IDEA FOR YOU...

The next time you find yourself in a group meeting where opinions are being sought, don't be shy: be willing to stand up and speak your mind. You might feel a little embarrassed at first, but with so few people willing to speak up, you will be noticed.

23 PERSEVERANCE

The truth is that if you truly want to succeed, you have to keep on going.

DEFINING IDEA...

Perseverance is the hard work you do after you get tired of doing the hard work you already did.

~ NEWT GINGRICH, US POLITICIAN

Von Clausewitz says little about perseverance. In fact he dedicates just three-quarters of a page to the subject. This is odd given the importance of perseverance in war, especially in the heat of the battle, but then he had a lot of other material to cover. However, what he does say is instructive – 'there is hardly a worthwhile enterprise in war whose execution does not call for infinite effort, trouble and privation; and as man under pressure tends to give in to physical and intellectual weakness, only great strength of will can lead to the objective. It is steadfastness that will earn the admiration of the world and posterity.' That sums up why perseverance matters so much. He didn't need to labour the point.

We should expect war and battles in particular to test the mettle of the combatants and if you've ever read about medieval battles you can see why: all those men, all that cutting and hacking, all those body parts. But plenty of non-violent examples demonstrate the critical quality of perseverance in everyday and business life. Take Roger Bannister, who despite the received wisdom at the time suggesting that breaking the 4-minute mile was not only impossible, but also bad for one's health, kept on practising until he finally achieved this. And you know what happened? He didn't suddenly drop dead of heart failure as the medics believed he would and then everyone else began breaking the 4-minute barrier too. Then there was Thomas Edison, who finally got to make a half-decent light bulb after years of trying and failing, 10,000 times in all. And don't forget Colonel Saunders, whose recipe for fried chicken was rejected on 1,009 occasions before the now-famous Kentucky Fried Chicken franchise was established. My favourite comes from the movie *The Untouchables* in which Elliot Ness (Kevin Costner) pits his wits against Al Capone (Robert De Niro). In one of the last scenes Ness goes up to Capone while he is being restrained in the courtroom (after his counsel changes his plea to guilty) and says, 'Never stop; never stop fighting until the fight is won.' And that sums up what perseverance is all about.

We all face our own Bannister, Edison or Ness moments in which we have a simple choice of persevering with something or giving up – major projects, a difficult sales opportunity and so on. Although it's tempting to quit when everyone is telling you it's impossible, or the challenge seems too great, it is far better to persevere. And as von Clausewitz points out so cogently it's steadfastness that earns admiration and posterity. Don't forget: no one remembers a loser.

HERE'S AN IDEA FOR YOU...

Look over your life and identify the times when you had to persevere (for example, at university, during a difficult project or even a sporting event). Try and recapture the feeling of achievement that you had when you finished the task. Even better, see if you can visualise it. Learn to bring these feelings and images back so that you can use them to help you get through your next major challenge.

24 CUNNING

Sometimes it is a good idea not to show your true hand too early.

DEFINING IDEA...

Cunning is the art of concealing our own defects, and discovering other people's weaknesses.

– WILLIAM HAZLITT, ENGLISH WRITER

Whenever someone talks about a colleague who is cunning, they usually refer to them as being as sly as a fox; they are considered underhand, devious and not to be trusted. But as von Clausewitz states when he addresses the subject of cunning in *On War*, all it implies is a secret purpose. He also makes the distinction between the use of cunning in normal life and that used in war. Whereas the former usually involves a breach of faith, the latter does not because there is none to be breached. So it is highly likely and indeed right that we might feel aggrieved in the normal course of events, but in war the use of cunning is fair game. And although cunning can be applied in war, because it confuses the enemy and forces them to make a mistake, it rarely occurs. Von Clausewitz makes it clear that often the price is too high because in order to fool the enemy the feint has to be very convincing and therefore requires a lot of planning and the use of manpower that might be required elsewhere. Moreover, there is always the risk that nothing will be gained from it.

So the question is: should we apply cunning in the business world? The only sensible answer is yes and no. At the business level, where you are locked in battle with your competitors, the answer might be yes, but it must be carefully applied as per von Clausewitz's advice. One apocryphal story springs to mind. After the Eiffel Tower was built (by the French, 984 ft) in 1889 it became the tallest structure in the world. However, the Americans were not going to stand for this. In the first few decades of the twentieth century a veritable skyscraper race began in New York. First came the Metropolitan Life Tower (700 ft), then the Woolworth Building (792 ft), quickly followed by the Bank of Manhattan Building (927 ft).

Then it was the turn of the competition between Craig Severance (who was busy building at 40 Wall Street) and Walter Chrysler, founder of the Chrysler Company, who was building elsewhere in Manhattan. As the buildings neared completion and were almost the same height, Severance quickly added a few extra floors and claimed the prize of having built the world's tallest building. But he didn't know that Chrysler (who had kept the intended height of his building a secret all along) had hidden a 185-ft-long spire inside the cone of his building. Once Severance claimed victory and downed tools, Chrysler had the spire hoisted and riveted into place, stealing the much-coveted prize from Severance.

It would be good to see the use of cunning outlawed. Unlike war or indeed competition between businesses, the breach of faith associated with cunning makes the whole thing more personal and therefore more damaging.

HERE'S AN IDEA FOR YOU...

Consider the use of cunning in your organisation. Visit the marketing division and review their campaigns. Is there anything they say or do that might be considered cunning when addressing their competition? Is it effective? How could the use of cunning be enhanced?

25 SURPRISE

Although it may be difficult to achieve in war it seems that many business executives are easily surprised.

DEFINING IDEA...

Whoever can surprise well,
must conquer.

– JOHN PAUL JONES, SCOTTISH-
BORN AMERICAN NAVAL HERO

Taking an enemy by surprise is one of the universal tenets of war. Surprise is the means of gaining superiority and whenever it is achieved on a grand scale it confuses the enemy and lowers their morale. The Blitzkrieg strategy of the German army in World War II did just that and it didn't take long for them to overrun the French as a result. There are other examples too, such as the 1918 spring offensive during the Great War and the Shock and Awe tactics of the Gulf War of 1990–1. However, back in von Clausewitz's era it wasn't so easy. Analysing the subject, he quite rightly points out that to surprise an enemy you need a combination of secrecy and speed, but to be successful you must have a high degree of energy on the part of the government and commander and a great deal of efficiency from the army. Needless to say, this was usually difficult to achieve and despite the near-universal desire to use surprise, von Clausewitz believed that by its very nature it could never be outstandingly successful. Ultimately the friction of war (decisions, mobilising troops, etc.) got in the way.

The importance and value of surprise in war is of course obvious, but what about business? In the corporate world, companies and the markets in general operate at a different speed to the military. The need for speed is still there but because it's not a life-or-death situation, things can afford to be a little bit more sedate, even pedestrian. However, so many business leaders, politicians and organisations are suddenly taken by surprise at the emergence of a new competitor or a disruptive technology. But such occurrences do not appear overnight: they take time to establish and usually, it must be said, in full view of the competition. This suggests it has less to do with genuine surprise, more ignorance, arrogance or the incompetence of those who lead businesses. For example, when Polaroid filed for bankruptcy in 2001 this was not due to the sudden appearance of digital photography but because the company had dismissed it out of hand and failed to recognise the legitimate threat. The same might be said of Microsoft, who refused to notice the threat from Netscape until it was too late (ironic, given their history with IBM). And when the markets collapsed at the start of the Credit Crunch, world leaders, bank CEOs and others went on record to state how surprised they were at the rapidity and severity of the events. Strange, many of us could see the car crash coming from some way off… Still, stupid is as stupid does.

HERE'S AN IDEA FOR YOU...

To avoid being taken by surprise, undertake a thorough risk review at the start of any major initiative. Although this might take time to complete and counter your usual desire to get on with the job, you'll avoid being tripped up by the 'OSINTOTs (Oh S***, I Never Thought of That!)' that trip so many others up.

26 MILITARY VIRTUES OF THE ARMY

A strong fighting unit and a successful organisation has one thing in common: a powerful *esprit de corps*.

DEFINING IDEA...

Every man's ability may be strengthened or increased by culture.

~ JOHN ABBOTT, AUTHOR

Military history tells us so much about how we behave, especially when under pressure, as it is only then that people's true colours are revealed. This is one reason why Steven Spielberg's *Band of Brothers* is so enjoyable to watch – powerful bonds develop within Easy Company as the series follows them from Normandy to the end of World War II. Such bonding was not lost on von Clausewitz, who believed military spirit to be one of the most important moral elements in war. If it is absent, not only must it be replaced by something else, such as a very strong leader, but it also results in inferior outcomes (mostly defeat, I guess). In his view an army that is able to maintain its cohesion under the most murderous of fire cannot be shaken by fear, resists with all its might and trusts and believes in its officers is imbued with military spirit. Such spirit inspired men on the Western Front during the Great War and citizens of London throughout the Blitz.

Organisations too need an *esprit de corps*, but unlike a crack military unit, it is less obvious how to capture the essence of this. That is why so much time and effort has been spent trying to unravel the nature of an organisation's culture. No matter what its size, each business has a particular way of working. Although we like to call this 'culture', it is in effect 'the way we do things round here' – the rules of engagement, so to speak. If you have changed jobs, worked abroad or perhaps consulted with different organisations, you will have noticed how they vary, even when doing ostensibly the same thing. The reason why they do this is because of their culture.

I remember when I was working in an investment bank on a Year 2000 programme for Ernst & Young. Like most banks, it was brash, loud and arrogant, and of course highly task-oriented and very different from E&Y. What I found interesting, though, was how new people would join the team and leave almost immediately. They were certainly smart enough to work there, but what they failed to do was to get into the way the bank operated and how the people interacted (its culture). There were no written rules, so it was hard and it certainly took me a while to figure it out. However, once I became a bit louder, ran roughshod over people and worried less about how they felt, I did just fine. Heck, they even tried to offer me a job! Culture really matters and although some organisations go out of their way to capture what it means in their core values, most do not. But its inclusion is to be recommended as understanding culture can be a lifesaver.

HERE'S AN IDEA FOR YOU...

What are the core values of your business? Are they written down and displayed around the office? If you don't know what they are, speak to people who have been in the company for some time or better still, consult HR. If you know what they are, make sure you embrace them as these can have a major impact on your career progression.

27 OTHER EMOTIONAL FACTORS

Not letting your emotions get the better of you can be difficult in war but it should be easy in the workplace, so long as you are emotionally intelligent.

DEFINING IDEA...

Human behaviour flows from three main sources: desire, emotion and knowledge.

~ PLATO, ANCIENT GREEK PHILOSOPHER

War is an emotional affair and evokes a range of responses from combatants and non-combatants alike, not least the classic fight-or-flight response. For von Clausewitz, the two key emotions in war are fear and courage. Fear is a basic response that all of us experience when faced with a dangerous situation, like being confronted by a ferocious lion, and is designed to preserve our physical being. Courage, however, is different in that it can override the natural feelings of anxiety when faced with danger, such as a cavalry charge. Incidentally this is something the Scots experienced at the Battle of Bannockburn in 1314; they held their ground against an English cavalry charge but only after practising for weeks beforehand so that they could override their natural instinct to run like crazy. Von Clausewitz considers courage to be the nobler instinct because it has the capability of neutralising the effects of danger. He makes the point that other emotions come into play but these only tend to show themselves in the higher ranks. Those who had to do the hard work of fighting were too busy grappling with the fear and courage seesaw to display much else. However, the higher ranks, nicely positioned half a mile from the battlefield, could afford to indulge in pride, humility, wrath, compassion, envy and generosity.

Fear and courage also play their part in working life. We all know how uncomfortable it can feel when faced with a difficult situation. Feelings of fear and anxiety may hold us back, but equally courage can spur us on. However, unlike war where the emotional responses are quite limited, at work we have to cope with a much wider range of feelings caused by such things as promotions, nightmare bosses, economic downturns, complex projects, high-maintenance employees and so on. It is clear from research that emotions can have a major impact on how effective we are at work, how we get on (or not) with our colleagues and at board level how well a business is managed. For example, it has been shown that the smartest people, who seemingly have little control over their emotional life, fare much worse in their careers and personal lives than those who have a balance between academic and emotional intelligence. No wonder there continues to be such a huge interest in emotional intelligence. There's no doubt that being emotionally intelligent allows us to be more self-aware, to manage the effects of our emotions more effectively, maintain our motivation under a range of circumstances, understand how others feel and manage relationships more deftly. Clearly being emotionally intelligent is an essential ingredient to long-term success, inside and outside work.

HERE'S AN IDEA FOR YOU...

Consider using some of the techniques associated with Neuro-linguistic Programming (NLP) to manage your emotional response to situations. The best way to do this is to apply the equation $E + R = O$ (Event + Response = Outcome). The next time you find yourself about to respond automatically, hold fire and think about how you can use your emotions to better effect and achieve the outcome you really want.

28 THE NATURE OF BATTLE TODAY

Keeping a close eye on what goes on on the ground can be an invaluable strategic tool.

DEFINING IDEA...

Strategy requires thought, tactics require observation.

~ MAX EUWE, DUTCH CHESS GRANDMASTER AND MATHEMATICIAN

Despite being a deep thinker, von Clausewitz was also a practical sort of guy, not surprising given that he fought in wars and experienced battle first-hand. This mix of thinking and doing, which tends to be rare in any walk of life, meant that he was able to translate the theory of war into practice and the practicalities of war into theory. When it came to the nature of the battle itself he was of the view that the strategy and tactics associated with its execution must be consistent – a truism perhaps, but an invaluable observation all the same. He also believed that if the tactical execution of battle should vary between engagements then it was probably time to review and update strategy. A good example of this was when the US 101st Airborne Division destroyed a battery of German 88 mm guns during the assault on Brécourt Manor in June 1944. This engagement took place shortly after D-Day and at the time there was no strategy for dealing with this type of situation. The tactics the soldiers developed to deal with the four guns was highly effective and they managed to disable the entire battery with very few casualties. More important, though, was that this approach became embedded in the strategic thinking of Allied Command.

There has always been an issue between strategic planning and business operations. Although an essential part of any sizable corporation, strategic planning constantly suffers from appearing too remote and disconnected.

Much of this is due to the strategy guys spending too little time on the operational front line of the business. Without this grounding, the strategies they produce, no matter how clever or forward thinking they might be, gain little or no traction and often fail to have any real impact. This reminds me of the time spent re-engineering the strategy and planning division in a UK government department. When I first arrived, I conducted a short review to assess how the division was perceived. It came as no surprise to discover they were not at all well respected and in many quarters were a bit of a laughing stock. Although bad, the situation was recoverable and considering the chairman and board were all for shutting the division down, my intervention couldn't have come at a better time. Reconnecting strategic planning with the business involved understanding the tactics currently being deployed across the organisation and working these into the strategic planning process. So instead of simply looking outside the department, it also meant looking inside too. Once developed, this required a heavy emphasis on operationalising the strategies, made possible by bringing the high-level project and programme planning function into the division. After 13 months of hard work they became a high-performing, grounded strategy function – just what every organisation needs.

HERE'S AN IDEA FOR YOU...

How is strategy developed and implemented in your business? In your opinion, is it grounded enough and is there sufficient emphasis on tactics? Visit your strategic planning function and ask them to describe their process and explore how it impacts your day-to-day work.

29 MUTUAL AGREEMENT TO FIGHT

Waiting until everyone is ready to fight may have been the done thing in the thirteenth century, but today conflict should wait for no one, especially if your very survival is at stake.

DEFINING IDEA...

Behold a contest worthy of a god, a brave man matched in conflict with adversity.

– SENECA, ROMAN PHILOSOPHER

'There can be no battle unless both sides are willing to engage in combat' – von Clausewitz was quick to point out that such a notion was outdated and failed to understand the true nature of modern warfare. In the past, the agreement to fight was an essential part of the process because to do so both sides had to find a suitable stretch of open ground on which to hack each other to death. It was impossible to fight set-piece battles anywhere else. In von Clausewitz's time, however, if a commander wanted to fight he could merely seek out his enemy and attack them; there was no requirement to ask first. Equally, if a commander wanted to retreat, he could do so and could not be forced into battle by his opponent, unless of course he found himself surrounded, but that was different. He was keen to emphasise that modern warfare is conducted within a broader strategic and political context, which means battles are part of a wider strategy, not just a test of strength.

Despite the received wisdom that conflict in the workplace is a bad thing, sometimes it is necessary to fight for the very survival of a company. In such instances nothing can be gained from waiting until there is a mutual agreement to fight. The battle has to be taken to the enemy and the person to do so is the CEO. One such guy is Willie Walsh, who runs British Airways. This is a man who is willing to take the battle wherever it needs to go to in order to save the airline he leads. British Airways, like many other airlines, has suffered terribly following the credit crisis and the onset of the Great Recession. Business-class passengers, on which the company depends for the bulk of their profits, have deserted them in their thousands. The investment banks and consultancies who thought nothing of sending teams to New York for an hour's meeting have booted out so many of their high-rolling employees that the business class cabins remain half-empty. And with such a dependence on high-paying customers, it should come as no surprise that the airline went from a record profit (in 2007) to a record loss in 2008: just 12 months! Walsh believes that unless drastic measures are taken, the company could go bust and any upturn in the economy will make little difference; the shifts in business travel will be permanent. Survival means many things to Walsh, not least attacking the remaining taboos in British Airways, such as the power of the cabin crews and pilots. If he wins the battle, we will still be able to fly with 'The World's Favourite Airline' – if not, it might just be easyJet!

HERE'S AN IDEA FOR YOU...

Look around your business. Are there practices, processes or taboos, which although not good for the company, are never tackled? What can you do to challenge them? Could you step up to the plate and bring some healthy conflict into the mix to address them?

30 ADVANCED GUARDS AND OUTPOSTS

Advanced guards and outposts are as essential to an army as research and development is to a business.

DEFINING IDEA...

We should favour innovation and freedom over regulation.

~ GEORGE ALLEN.
AMERICAN FOOTBALL COACH

Von Clausewitz believed the use of advanced guards and outposts was one of the few areas of military doctrine where the threads of strategy and tactics were interwoven. As a separate fighting unit operating some distance away from the main army, they were a crucial link in the chain of strategy and often vital in ensuring the tactical battle plan was carried out effectively. He also points out that any army not completely battle-ready had to have an advanced guard in order to find out what the enemy was up to; without them they could end up fighting blind, something no commander in his right mind would want.

From one perspective at least the research and development function might be viewed as the business equivalent of von Clausewitz's advanced guards and outposts. They too form a crucial link in the chain of strategy in that they can take the ideas and concepts developed by the strategists and test them out first before they are productionised. Also, they have a role to play in the tactical implementation of new products because they can help get the ball rolling. I saw this first-hand when I used to interface into the research and development function of Ordnance Survey, the UK's national mapping agency. The guys were great fun to work with and brilliant at translating strategic concepts into prototype products. My job was to convert these into robust and saleable products by productionising their prototypes. This was not an easy task because Research and Development didn't have to follow the same standards and processes as me. However, I'm certain that they would not have been half as successful had they done this, so I shouldn't complain.

Smart companies clearly understand that when used wisely, research and development adds significant value to the bottom line. For example, Procter & Gamble (P&G) currently employs cave technology to accelerate their market research. This allows P&G to create virtual reality stores mirroring the shops of their customers, such as Tesco, Sainsbury and Boots, in every detail. The 'cave' environment means customers and clients can walk through the store, handle the merchandise and even buy individual products. P&G is using the reactions of customers who use the cave technology to test alternative store layouts, displays and even packaging, which is helping them to dramatically accelerate the pace of innovation and cut costs while working to win over powerful retail clients. The process, which usually takes up to two years to complete, can now be wrapped up within three months

Having a vibrant research and development function is central to the innovation process and although this has always been the case, the nature of competition today means the function is more important than ever.

HERE'S AN IDEA FOR YOU...

How are new ideas, products and services nurtured in your company? Are they given enough space to flourish or crushed by too much process or lack of interest? Analyse how innovation is managed in other organisations, such as pharmaceutical companies, to see how you compare. What can you learn and how might you be more innovative in your day-to-day work?

31 OPERATIONAL USE OF ADVANCED CORPS

Used well, the Advanced Corps can tell you plenty about your enemy. Equally, when used well, consultants can reveal a lot about your organisation.

DEFINING IDEA...

In every society some men are born to rule, and some to advise.

~ RALPH WALDO EMERSON, US ESSAYIST

In von Clausewitz's time the task of the Advanced Corps was to observe the enemy and slow down its advance. However, there was an ulterior motive: they were also expected to induce the enemy to deploy their full resources and therefore reveal their intentions. This was possible so long as the enemy was on the move and the advanced guard had ample opportunity to observe enemy forces and retreat when things got out of hand. Ultimately, in von Clausewitz's opinion, the Advanced Corps derived its operational value from its presence, not its efforts. One might argue the same is true of management consultants.

Over the years, management consultancy has had lots of bad press. Characters like Alan Sugar and Martin Sorrell refuse to use them, believing they are little more than parasites. Others laugh at the classic quip – give a consultant your watch and they will tell you the time. Then there's the T-shirt: 'I'm not unemployed, I'm a consultant'. Much of the poor image is down to consultants stating the obvious, preparing reports and presentations packed full of foam-inducing jargon, generating recommendations that are impossible to implement and screwing up major projects. Sure, there are some bad consultants out there with little more than an amoeba for a brain but some very good ones too. And we must remember that organisations are often appalling at managing consultants once they have been allowed through the door (a bit like vampires, perhaps), so on that basis some of the problems rest with the clients too.

If we were to view consultants as the latter-day Advanced Corps, maybe we could not only get more value out of them but also deploy them to greater effect. Many organisations like to use consultants to deliver bad news or take the sting out of the change process as they can be blamed for recommending the change. Of course this is fine, but remember what von Clausewitz says about presence and efforts. It is far better to use hired hands to draw out the concerns and issues the organisation might have about change than to get them to implement it. This ensures the presence of the consultants can be used to provide the vital independent sounding board for staff and in so doing encourage their true feelings and intentions to surface – important, if change is to be successful. It also avoids many of the disasters associated with letting armies of consultants loose on the business; often their efforts can tie it up in knots. No doubt if von Clausewitz was a modern-day CEO he wouldn't dismiss consultants out of hand but would use them expertly.

HERE'S AN IDEA FOR YOU...

Most probably your company uses consultants from time to time and it is worth understanding how and why they are used. Spend some time with those who have used consultants and find out how they maximised their value. And if the opportunity presents itself, ask to spend some time with consultants to see first-hand how they operate.

32 CONCENTRATION OF FORCES IN SPACE

Focusing your forces onto one objective makes perfect sense in war and it pays off in business too.

DEFINING IDEA...

The whole world steps aside for the man who knows where he is going.

~ ANON

Von Clausewitz always believed the best strategy in war was to be very strong. In his opinion, the most obvious way to do this was to concentrate your forces in one place and not allow them to drift apart. Unfortunately there were too many instances of armies being divided and separated without reason; often it must be said because the commander felt that it would be a good idea. Invariably this wasn't the case and von Clausewitz was adamant the only way to avoid such folly was to drum the criticality of the concentration of forces into the minds of the military leadership so that they would do this automatically. Reading about General Kitchener's attempt to rescue General Gordon from Khartoum in 1898, which involved his men fighting in tightly formed squares from the north of the country against hordes of Dervishes, it becomes clear why it makes sense to keep your forces concentrated.

New York is one of the few American cities where walking is both easy and encouraged. And as you stroll, you will notice that there is a Starbucks on virtually every block, sometimes more than one. From a von Clausewitzian perspective they have clearly concentrated their forces in space. Starbucks has been quite deliberate in doing this because it allows them to draw custom away from existing coffee shops. Even when they have set up so many stores in a city that there are no more customers to draw away, new branches are opened. The reason why they choose to do this is because they would rather cannibalise their own clientele than allow the competition any wiggle room whatsoever.

What is interesting is that although the competing franchises may suffer a reduction in custom, this tends to be short-lived. Within a few weeks, or perhaps a couple of months, both stores run at full capacity. It seems that having a greater number of stores brings in more customers. Such success seems a long way away from when Starbucks first started, back in Seattle, Washington, in 1971. Its dream was to transform the coffee drinking experience of the average American by combining high-quality coffee with the charm and romance of the European coffee house. Although doubtful whether it could ever replace the charm of a Parisian coffee shop, it has certainly been phenomenally successful: its stock price increased by 5,000% between 1987 and 2006, and the number of employees grew from 100 to 100,000 over the same period. Four million coffee drinks are now sold each day in the US alone. Despite suffering in the recession, Starbucks refuses to budge from the strategy of concentrating its stores and that kind of attitude means continued success.

HERE'S AN IDEA FOR YOU...
How well do you use all the resources available to you when you need to get something done? Are you aware of what you can draw on, within and outside your team? Find out what resources you have at hand and think about how you can use them in the future. Even better, note them for future reference.

33 UNIFICATION OF FORCES IN TIME

The old adage 'Too many cooks spoil the broth' applies to both the army and the office, but sometimes everything must be brought to bear to finish the job.

DEFINING IDEA...

Get the job done.

~ DON SHULA, AMERICAN
FOOTBALL COACH

Reading *On War* is a little like wading through treacle – it's really hard going! At times, it seems to me that all we get is a stream of consciousness rather than carefully constructed argument, as is the case when von Clausewitz discusses the importance of the unification of forces in time. His main argument is actually quite simple and focuses on whether it's best to throw all your men into an engagement at once or hold some back ready to join when really needed. Having a few hundred men in reserve is a good thing as they will be fresh and battle-ready; if their side is losing, however, it won't make any difference to the outcome. Von Clausewitz believes this dilemma is only a problem during the initial phases of the battle and reflects the fundamental difference between strategy and tactics. After some consideration, he feels it is more appropriate to act strategically. In his view it is far better to apply all your forces simultaneously: their effectiveness will be far greater because everything can be concentrated in a single action in a single moment in time. As Nike says, 'Just Do It.'

In 1998 I was involved in a year 2000 programme at a global investment bank. Like so many institutions then, they were concerned that the date change from 1999 to 2000 would spell business Armageddon. Millions were poured into thousands of projects across the world and my job was to pull them together and generate a bi-weekly report to key people in the bank.

As you might suspect, many thousands were working on the programme and keeping everyone focused on something that was in the main very dull and boring was a real struggle at times. As the bank had started quite late compared to most others, it lagged behind. And as time went on the gap between where they needed to be and where they actually were became ever wider. Slipping the deadline wasn't going to work and if they really wanted to be out of a job at the beginning of the year all they had to do was continue the way they were. In the end the project managers and business leaders got it; the bank got it too and, as the deadline loomed, everyone suddenly focused on the job in hand and successfully completed the programme. Year 2000 came and went without a hitch and everybody went back to their day jobs. They had unified their forces at the right time and thrown everything they had at the problem. It was strategically perfect, if occasionally tactically erratic.

HERE'S AN IDEA FOR YOU...

Separating the urgent from the important is a key skill for a busy executive. Can you do this? The best way to manage all the things you have to do is to start the day by separating tasks: important but not urgent, important and urgent, urgent but not important and not important or urgent. This allows you to prioritise your workload and makes you highly productive.

34 THE STRATEGIC RESERVE

Balancing the need to hold men back with the need to commit them to battle is difficult. In business the same can be said of finance.

DEFINING IDEA...
But we can't deploy everything. We would have to use prudence in how we share our resources.
~ LISA RAY, ACTRESS

According to von Clausewitz, the Reserve has two purposes: the first to prolong and renew fighting, in essence to push home a victory when needed and overwhelm the enemy; the other to counter any unforeseen threats, such as being overrun on the right flank. However, he was clear that the concept of a strategic reserve had little or no place in military strategy. In fact, he believed that the Reserve was positioned for tactical use only and unequivocal that the idea of maintaining a strategic reserve becomes less essential, less useful and far more dangerous to employ, the more inclusive and general its intended purpose. In conclusion, he states that it is an absurdity to maintain a strategic reserve that is not meant to contribute to an overall decision.

A few months ago, I was having a coffee with a CFO of a major listed company and we were discussing the state of the markets, specifically how the investment analysts had suddenly switched their opinion about corporate debt. For a long time they had frowned on companies that were prudent and sat on significant cash piles; they were considered pariahs, unadventurous and not doing enough for their shareholders. Clearly of the same mind as von Clausewitz – if you are not going to use the cash for something, why keep it?

The advice these geniuses dished out was that it was better to binge on corporate debt; buy back shares and become highly leveraged than sit on a solid cash reserve. Almost overnight they changed their opinion and crucified any company with too much debt. The CFO had been persuaded by company analysts to take on more debt to acquire a European company yet a few weeks later he was taken to task at the AGM for being too highly geared by the very same people. The problem with analysts is they don't tend to know what they're talking about.

Today, however, there can no doubt that the availability of credit will be constrained for quite some time, which means that those businesses with good cash flows, excellent balance sheets and plenty of reserves are in a strong position. Companies like Pfizer, Microsoft, Corning and Bausch & Lomb will not only be able to weather the economic storm but enhance their market positions as a result. And although this may go against the military doctrine espoused by von Clausewitz, so long as they use their cash reserves to advance their market position, I'm sure he would forgive them.

HERE'S AN IDEA FOR YOU...

Having some kind of reserve be it money or people can be extremely helpful when times get tough. Consider the types of events that you might need to respond to, which could be considered out of the ordinary, then determine what you would need to respond to them effectively. Assess what resources you might need to hold in reserve to manage them, should they arise.

35 MAXIMUM USE OF FORCE

Wars are never won by being nice to each other. At times being in business also requires us to behave as though we are at war and winning usually means using everything we have in our armoury.

Von Clausewitz made it very clear in his first book that war was a messy business with no point in pussyfooting around. In his view, being kind-hearted and intellectual about it all and trying to figure out how to disarm an enemy without bloodshed was pointless and would only end in tears, if not complete annihilation. War was about the maximum use of force.

Of course it might be argued that the world of work is very different from an eighteenth-century battlefield, but sometimes work resembles war and in such instances we really should follow von Clausewitz's advice. In those instances where your personal or corporate survival is at stake it might be nice to treat people with the respect they deserve, but being ruthless and putting niceties aside is generally the better strategy.

Every year in the UK we are subjected to *The Apprentice*, a TV programme in which sixteen candidates are pitched together in a series of somewhat unrealistic and arguably pointless assignments in order to impress leading entrepreneur Alan Sugar and become his apprentice. In each of the episodes, set over twelve weeks, one of the apprentices is fired by Lord Sugar in a boardroom showdown. It is here where you see those who follow the von Clausewitz School of Charm: those who are ruthless use the boardroom as a forum for crushing the competition while the thoughtful caring types are discarded with their egos, ambitions and TV careers in tatters. Perhaps not a good advertisement for the workforce or indeed apprentices in general, but you know, it's kind of realistic – especially when a pay cheque of £100,000 is being offered as the prize.

Between October and November 1998 one of the largest leveraged buyouts in American history took place when Kohlberg, Kravis & Roberts (KKR) took control of RJR Nabisco. This messy affair started when Nabisco, after taking advice from KKR, decided to pursue a management buyout backed by investment bank Shearson Lehman Hutton and its parent company, American Express. Not to be outdone, and with Nabisco firmly in their sights, KKR made a counter offer and used every tactic under the sun to secure the deal. Despite the great and the good on Wall Street piling into the battle, KKR won out because of their ruthless focus and the maximum use of force, which in 1988 extended to institutional investors, pension funds and the Harvard University endowment. What ultimately swung it was the board, who really didn't want to see CEO Joss Johnson walk away with $100 m, which he would have received from a rival bidder. In some ways, *The Apprentice* and Nabisco are very similar – and both make great television.

HERE'S AN IDEA FOR YOU...

Imagine a situation where your career or company may be under threat from a rival. Jot down on a piece of paper what you would do to prevent that rival from succeeding (keeping it legal, of course). You might be surprised at just how far you might go.

36 RELATIVE STRENGTH

Gaining the upper hand, both in war and in business is less about size, more about competitive and comparative advantage. So, what's yours?

DEFINING IDEA...

If you don't have competitive advantage, don't compete.

– JACK WELCH, FORMER CEO OF GE

For a long time battles have been won on the basis of numerical superiority; when two sides came together, it was usually the one with the greatest number of men that won. Sometimes a smaller force took to the field and annihilated their enemy, such as at Agincourt in 1415, but in the main it really was a case of size does matter. Today of course such maxims of war have been replaced with the relative advantage achieved through the effective use of technology, so having more men no longer means success is guaranteed. Von Clausewitz was writing at a time when many were of the view that the superiority of numbers was becoming more, not less important. However, he believed otherwise and considered the relative strength of an army to be more crucial. The reason for this was that the armies of his day were very much alike in terms of weapons, training and equipment, and as a result well matched. This meant that even a small advantage could go a long way towards winning a battle.

It is possible to translate von Clausewitz's notion of relative strength into competitive and comparative advantage. The former is critical for an individual company, while the latter is more important at a regional level and typified by Detroit, which used to have comparative advantage in the automobile market. Following the Credit Crunch, most car manufacturers have suffered terribly, with much of the comparative advantage lost to Asian companies such as Toyota. Plus, of course, no one wants to buy Hummers anymore – with a petrol consumption of around a gallon per mile, no one can afford to run them.

Competitive advantage can be achieved in many different ways: some companies use technology, others innovation, while many choose to beat the competition on price (most notably Wal-Mart). Fortunately Michael Treacy and Fred Wiersema, authors of *The Discipline of Market Leaders*, have given us a simple lens with which to view competitive advantage. In their model they believe there are three ways in which companies can gain the upper hand over rivals. The first is by becoming operationally excellent where the organisation is able to deliver a combination of quality, price and ease of purchase that no one in their market can match. Examples include CostCo and Ryanair. The next is through product leadership. Organisations pursuing this approach do so by continually pushing their products so that they are always desirable and at the leading edge. They are experts at innovation and bringing new products to market. Examples include Johnson & Johnson and, of course, Apple. The final way which companies gain advantage is by becoming customer intimate. Those adopting this approach deliver whatever their customers want and are expert at mass customisation and outside innovation (having their customers help define their products for them). Examples include Lego and Dell.

HERE'S AN IDEA FOR YOU...

Find out what's unique about your company and how this translates into competitiveness. Consider how what you do (and your team, if you have one) helps achieve this and what else you might do to make it even more powerful.

37 SUPERIORITY OF NUMBERS

Big can be beautiful, but when it comes to the numbers game the question is: are you using your resources wisely?

When von Clausewitz discusses the effect which superiority of numbers has on war he does so only on the basis of having stripped out all the other factors associated with strategy and tactics first.

His argument is that without a good strategy and excellent tactics, we are left with nothing more than a shapeless battle in which the only distinguishing factor is the number of troops on either side. He also points out that having more men may ultimately contribute very little to the outcome of an engagement and will only do so if the numbers are great enough to counterbalance the strategy and tactics of their opponents. In other words, although it is essential to field as large a force as possible, it's crucial to use the superiority of numbers to good effect.

I'm not a great fan of shopping – all that senseless pushing around with oversized bags and overpriced tripe; it's to be avoided as much as possible! Funny, though, I don't mind shopping at supermarkets so much: at least they are cool and I can use the trolley as a lethal weapon. Tesco is a fine example of superiority in numbers in action. The supermarket wars in the UK have raged on for years while Tesco, Sainsbury's, Asda and Morrisons slug it out for the top slot. Tesco has been able to capture and hold onto the top position for a long time now. Although size certainly makes a difference, it has been the way that it uses this to invest in new technology and ideas that has made the difference. One area in particular really stands out: their Clubcard customer loyalty scheme. Piloted back in 1993, the card was rolled out nationally in 1994 in the belief that it could deliver more than just a boost to like-for-like sales. Tesco was looking for an increase in customer goodwill and ultimately in loyalty. Rather than forcing customers to take their rewards at the checkout as Sainsbury's did, they personalised it and allowed customers to use the benefits how they liked. The initial results were amazing; far better than they hoped for, with over 80% of daily sales coming from Clubcard members. By May 2006, over £80 m was being paid to Tesco customers every quarter. Today vouchers can be spent on food, plus a whole range of non-food items including books, magazines, holidays and family days out, film hire and a whole lot more. This has left its competitors trailing.

I like to view von Clausewitz's superiority of numbers in much broader terms and, for the business world, this really translates into superiority of resources, be that cash flow, talented staff, application of technology or top-notch customer loyalty. On all counts, Tesco wins.

HERE'S AN IDEA FOR YOU...

How well do you use the resources (budget, staff, etc.) available to you? What changes might you introduce to make even better use of them? When considering the changes, be sure to involve your staff (if you have any) – they are bound to have some great ideas.

38 THE DYNAMIC LAW

Just as night follows day, periods of equilibrium are followed by times of tension. Although we can't do much about this, we can ensure that our decision-making is up to par when it matters.

DEFINING IDEA...

In any moment of decision the best thing you can do is the right thing, the next best thing is the wrong thing, and the worst thing you can do is nothing.

~ THEODORE ROOSEVELT, US PRESIDENT

In Book Three, von Clausewitz talks about the dynamic law in which periods of active warfare are interspersed with rest. Although it is obvious that an army cannot fight without rest for long (unless they happen to be terminators, of course), it is the significance of the decisions made during the two periods that was of particular interest to von Clausewitz. He believed that the importance of any decision was always greater during periods of tension than equilibrium. In equilibrium armies were neither attacking nor defending, they were just, well, being armies – moving around, polishing their bayonets and generally making a nuisance of themselves with the local population. This makes sense as the consequences of a decision, even a poor one, have less of an impact when things are ticking along. However, when making a decision when tensions are running high, it had better be a good one because the impacts can be immense.

The gaming world, and in particular games consoles, is a prime example of the business equivalent of von Clausewitz's dynamic law in practice. For a long time, games consoles were pretty similar: the same concept, similar handsets and near-identical games. The principal area of competition between the main players, Nintendo, Microsoft and Sony, focused on speed and graphics. Each would develop faster processors and launch new and improved consoles to gain or regain the top slot. Game companies would follow by producing more complex games, the latest generation of which are incredibly lifelike.

Despite this constant leapfrogging, the market was in equilibrium. There was nothing consequential about the new consoles; it was very much a case of more of the same. Eventually, this comfortable equilibrium gave way to a degree of tension; the market was becoming saturated, with nowhere to go. Finally, it was Nintendo who made the bold move to launch the Wii in 2006. Taking a radical departure, the Wii was not only wireless, but designed to appeal to the non-traditional gaming market: old people, the middle-aged and women who were never into games that much, if at all. It wasn't really geared to stereotypical spotty, socially stunted youths who spend all day in their rooms. In any case, the graphics on the Nintendo would never be a match for their favourite consoles. To increase the appeal, Nintendo introduced a degree of physicality into their games and as a result, realism. So, when you are playing tennis you actually swing the racquet; you can even do keep fit using the Wii board – a boon to the overweight and gym-haters everywhere.

HERE'S AN IDEA FOR YOU...

Observe the decision makers in your organisation. Try and understand how they make their decisions. In particular, see if you can see any difference to their decision-making styles in times of equilibrium and tension. What can you learn and apply to your own decision-making process?

39 WAR PLANS

If you want to do something well, you had better plan well.

DEFINING IDEA...

A riot is a spontaneous outburst. A war is subject to advance planning.

– RICHARD NIXON, US PRESIDENT

A long time ago I used to work alongside the Royal Engineers. One thing that always impressed me was their ability to plan – those guys could organise surveys across an entire country and execute them flawlessly. When I quizzed one of the Staff Sergeants on how they did it, all he said was the following: 'Planning and preparation prevents piss-poor performance.' This statement, also known as The Six Ps in polite company, sums up the importance and centrality of planning to all they did. Von Clausewitz was also a great fan of planning and believed that war plans should cover every aspect of conflict, weaving them into a single operation with an ultimate objective. In his view, no one should start a war without fully understanding what they intended to achieve by it (the political purpose) and how they intended to conduct it (the operational objective). This and only this would set the course of what was to follow, define the scale and effort required to prosecute the war and influence the smallest operational detail. In most cases, the purpose of war was to defeat the enemy and take over some, or all of their country, although sometimes all that was necessary was to give the enemy a bloody nose so they would never bother you again.

The Six Ps has stayed with me throughout my career and provides plenty of amusement in a planning session. I like to think of them as the equivalent of McKinsey's Seven-S model, but better. Given that planning is an essential component to every business, you might have thought they would be good at it by now. Unfortunately most corporations are quite poor at planning and as a result their execution often leaves a lot to be desired. I have read many reports decrying the lack of planning in projects and businesses in general and so I was delighted when I came across Isochron. This is a company that takes planning as seriously as von Clausewitz and follows his principle of the ultimate objective.

According to Isochron, the secret to good planning is to start with the outcome in mind and work backwards from it, to live the plan in reverse. Although perhaps counterintuitive, it really works and gets away from the problems associated with starting at the beginning and working to the end – dead ends, wasted effort, duplication and so on. Starting at the end and working backwards you can build an efficient plan that only deals with the things that really matter, which support the ultimate objective (nothing more, nothing less). And it doesn't matter whether you are planning a takeover, a new product launch or a major systems implementation, this can be applied to anything, even war.

HERE'S AN IDEA FOR YOU...

What kind of plans do you need to produce in your job? Are they comprehensive and do they cover all bases in the same way as The Six Ps suggest? Review how you develop and execute your plans then identify areas where your planning process might be improved.

40 CRITICAL ANALYSIS

Getting to the root cause of both success and failure is an essential skill if you are to remain successful and avoid the mistakes of the past.

DEFINING IDEA...

Get the habit of analysis – analysis will in time enable synthesis to become your habit of mind.

~ FRANK LLOYD WRIGHT,
AMERICAN ARCHITECT AND WRITER

There's no doubt that von Clausewitz was a clever guy and to synthesise so much of what he saw about him as he went through his military career was quite some feat. But his analysis is second to none and when he turns his attention to the specific nature of critical analysis, he hits the nail right on the head. He understands the value of analysis in general, but also the need to apply judgement when completing it. In his opinion, critical analysis consists of the discovery and interpretation of equivocal facts, tracing effects back to their root cause and the investigation and evaluation of means employed. In other words, taking the trouble to find out why something succeeds or fails by investigating the underlying factors and behaviours of those involved. Von Clausewitz also recognises that it can be very difficult to separate cause from effect, not surprising when you are at war, with bullets flying everywhere.

We have to remember that von Clausewitz didn't have the range of analysis tools and techniques that we do today, which makes our analysis much richer than his and hopefully more valuable. What is interesting, though, is that although we might be better at analysis, we are usually poor at learning from it. I think that's because unless we are learning first-hand and through direct experience, we tend to ignore the advice, input and theories of others. Humankind can be foolish in this way, which probably explains why, despite all the analysis, many dismiss the dangers of global warming.

There is one technique which seems to work exceptionally well, however, and that's the After Action Review (AAR). The After Action Review originated during the Vietnam War, when the soldiers in the field knew more than the generals at headquarters. This technique allows people to learn immediately after an event, irrespective of success or failure; the key thing is that it takes place immediately. Conducting an After Action Review takes between 20 and 30 minutes and is designed to answer the following questions: What should have happened? What actually happened? What are the differences between the two? What lessons can be drawn from the experience? How can any strengths revealed be built upon, any weaknesses reduced or eliminated? It's a very powerful technique: since its origination in the US Army, it has been successfully applied to industry by many well-known companies, including BP, where it is part and parcel of their organisational learning ethos.

My favourite technique, though, is the good old Ishikawa or cause and effect/ fishbone diagram. It's so simple to use and makes the whole process of critical analysis interactive, highly valuable – and, dare I say it, fun.

HERE'S AN IDEA FOR YOU...

The next time you're engaged in a problem-solving activity, use some of the many critical analysis tools available, such as After Action Reviews, GE Workouts and root cause analysis. Ideally you should complete this in a workshop environment – the results tend to be much better as a result.

41 FRICTION IN WAR

What appears to be relatively simple on paper often turns out to be very difficult in reality.

DEFINING IDEA...

The more I practise, the luckier I get.
– GARY PLAYER, SOUTH AFRICAN GOLFER

Several years ago I was coached by a partner at one of the 'Big Four' professional firms: the guy was not particularly likeable – he wasn't a good coach and had a 'little-big man' complex. Having heard that I had written a couple of books, he felt the need to tell how easy it was – just 200 pages of text and that was that. I tried to enlighten him, but to no avail. I'm sure if he ever attempted to write a book himself, he would realise that it wasn't quite so easy. This difference between theory and practice, or what is written on paper and what happens in reality is what von Clausewitz termed 'friction'. Friction in war comes from a variety of sources, including the weather, terrain, enemy action, the behaviour of the troops and so on. In his opinion, 'everything in war is very simple, but the simplest thing is difficult'. He believed that until you had experienced war and understood how difficulties could accumulate to make a straightforward task an impossible one, it was hard to comprehend. Indeed, seemingly minor incidents that could never have been foreseen often combine to reduce performance so that it falls short of the intended goal. Von Clausewitz believed only iron will could smash through such obstacles and still succeed.

Executing a project or running a business looks easy on paper, but until you've attempted either, it is difficult to comprehend the type of obstacles you will face. Just as in war, friction serves to slow things down and makes them a lot harder than you would be led to believe when reading a book or listening to a lecture at business school. In the corporate world, friction comes from a broad set of factors, including internal politics, personal ambition, customers, staff, bosses and of course, technology. In many organisations, getting things done often takes longer and involves a lot more pain than you might think, especially something so significant as Westpac's CS90 project. When the Australian banking system was deregulated in 1984, Westpac saw a massive opportunity and in 1987 launched the CS90 project. At a cost of A\$100 m, it was designed to allow them to compete globally. Expectations were high, but what looked good on paper failed to work well in practice. After 5 years and becoming A\$50 m over budget, the project was canned. Though feasible from a technical perspective, it suffered from the friction that derails so many major initiatives: the corporate culture got in the way, their business partner (IBM) failed to adapt to the Westpac way of doing things, internal politics caused major delays, bank staff resisted the change and the project was poorly controlled. Like war, until you have experienced such a nightmare you won't believe it could ever happen. Unfortunately it does, and all too often.

HERE'S AN IDEA FOR YOU...

Before you attempt anything new, such as running a project, launching a new product and so on, consider what might go wrong. So many people assume that things will work first time that they are surprised when they don't. Don't be similarly fooled: work with those around you to identify potential pitfalls and more importantly, use these to inform your planning.

42 INTELLIGENCE IN WAR

Intelligence reports in war are contradictory, false and out of date and the same is true in corporations. Cutting through the crap to get to what really matters was hard in von Clausewitz's time because there wasn't much of it, but it's even harder today.

DEFINING IDEA...

We should not only use the brains we have, but all that we can borrow.

– WOODROW WILSON, US PRESIDENT

Von Clausewitz's view of intelligence was really focused on information and lots of it. Well, as much as they could muster back in the late eighteenth and early nineteenth centuries when there was no internet and few people had cell phones. Although he recognised that good and reliable information was the bedrock of superior intelligence, he understood that the majority of it was conflicting, unreliable, probably false and most likely out of date. Despite this he felt that all information could be helpful so long as it was used carefully. Key to this was the ability, experience and judgement of the person receiving and using the information. Unsurprisingly he warned against the novice or inexperienced commander, who would often misinterpret it all and make the wrong decision.

Over the years, and especially since the introduction of computers in the workplace, the availability of information has grown exponentially. This has led us to believe that because we have lots of information, we will somehow be better at decision-making. Let's face it: anyone can get hold of whatever information they need in the desired format (sliced, diced and served up on a bed of lettuce, if they want), that's the power of integrated systems. But just as in von Clausewitz's time, it is how this information is used and assessed that really matters. Despite all the information swilling around the typical corporation (trillions of bits of data, according to some commentators), few are good at understanding, interpreting or using it wisely. In addition, more information does not make someone a better decision maker; in fact the opposite is often true. Too many executives have become information junkies and cannot make a decision unless they have every last piece of relevant data. Without a filter, they fall into the same trap as the novice commander 150 years ago.

The best decisions are always made in the absence of total information; in other words, they are carried out with the application of judgement. I like to call this intelligent intelligence, because even in today's information-rich, technology enabled corporation much of what is available is unreliable, out of date and very often false. No change since the 1780s then. The difference today, of course, is that everyone seems to be more than happy to use such tools as the free encyclopaedia *Wikipedia* as their primary source of accurate and reliable information. Although there's a lot to merit the wisdom of crowds, this isn't an intelligent way to gather useful information, which probably explains why the US military is returning to human intelligence. Ultimately, you just can't beat it.

HERE'S AN IDEA FOR YOU...

The next time you're preparing a report or perhaps a strategic document, consider whether the information you are using is unreliable, out of date, false or inaccurate. Before you finalise it, think how it will be used and cut out anything that could cloud the key message. As the old adage goes, less is more.

43 THE BATTLE: ITS DECISION

A project is like a battle – the only objective is to succeed, but success is never guaranteed.

DEFINING IDEA...

Change is not made without inconvenience, even from worse to better.

~ SAMUEL JOHNSON,
ENGLISH LEXICOGRAPHER

Never one to overcomplicate things, von Clausewitz always breaks down the essence of war into basic building blocks, which explains why *On War* is so large. But, like maths, it helps to get to grips with basic arithmetic before attempting double integration. When he turns his attention to the battle itself, he makes it clear that more than any other type of action in war the battle exists purely for its own sake. And if this is the case, the elements of its decision must be contained within it. In other words, victory must be pursued so long as it lies within the realm of possibility and battle should never be abandoned because of individual circumstances or events, but only when the available strength is no longer adequate. For a commander in the field, this means paying attention to a few important signs: the psychological impact of the commanding officer's moral stamina, the rate at which troops are lost compared to the enemy and how much ground has been lost. If all these look bad, it's highly likely the battle will be lost.

For well over 20 years, I have been involved with projects of one kind or another and when you think about it, a project has many of the same qualities as a battle. They are designed to be successful (after all, why undertake them in the first place if you expect to fail?), the decisions must be contained within it (in other words, no need for meddling busybodies like Internal Audit to poke their noses in) and the project should always be pursued so long as success remains in the realm of possibility (having the courage to finish the job even when it gets a little tough). Like any battle, the outcome is always uncertain and success cannot be guaranteed. Indeed, there are plenty of failed projects out there and some are extremely costly – the Child Support Agency's system (£456 m) and Denver City airport's automated baggage handling system (too large to mention, especially as they have now reverted back to manual baggage handling) are just two. That's why we need trained project managers, as well as solid project management disciplines. And in the same way that there are a few important signs that a commander in the field has to keep his eye on, so too does the project manager. In this case, it's progress against plan, spend against budget, team morale, stakeholder commitment and that old chestnut that most tend to forget: the delivery of the benefits. Of course there's one key distinction: most commanders know when to quit. Unfortunately most project managers refuse to do so and continue to flog a dead horse long after the battle has been well and truly lost – something the UK government does all the time!

HERE'S AN IDEA FOR YOU...

The next time you're involved in a project consider the key elements of success and failure; document them and develop a simple performance monitoring approach that allows you to judge whether the project will be a success. Use this to manage your stakeholders and maintain support.

44 DURATION OF THE ENGAGEMENT

How long a military engagement lasts depends on whether you are attacking or defending; the length of a sale depends on how desperate you are!

DEFINING IDEA...

The sale begins when the customer says yes.

~ HARVEY MACKAY,
MOTIVATIONAL SPEAKER

Von Clausewitz believed that the duration of a military engagement could be considered a separate, secondary success. The decision to cease fighting can never be reached too soon for the victor and delayed too long for the vanquished. Even back then, presumably, it was possible to spin the outcome any way you wanted. And let's face it: it always looks good on the commander if he manages to defeat the enemy in a swift engagement. By the same reckoning, it also reflects well if he and his men put up a spirited defence before capitulating. In both cases, the commander can walk away with a degree of honour and respect, even getting an extra medal or two to pin on his chest in the process. Of course, for the troops, things were a little different: being on the winning side usually meant that you were still alive, while the losing side guaranteed you were a corpse.

On reflection, the sales process is very similar. On one side you have the salesperson armed with their product or service that they want to sell and on the other is the potential client, who is often in no particular hurry to buy anything and needs persuading. Like the victor and the vanquished, the salesperson wants to close the deal as quickly as possible and the client prefers to draw it out. Both can get great kudos as a result. The guy who closes a big deal in double-quick time looks like a hero and the client who draws out the sale, getting a big discount along the way, is seen as a brilliant negotiator.

So, there you have it: the sales process is a bit of a game with both sides vying to come out as the true victor in the engagement. The question we must ask ourselves, though, is how long should the sales process last? Unlike a military engagement, which rarely lasts more than a few hours, the sales cycle can go on for weeks, months and sometimes years. Naturally the nature of the sale, the potential prize, the number of people involved and the culture of the buying organisation all have a bearing, but sometimes continually pushing a sale is like flogging a dead horse. I'm a great fan of the sales funnel in which you capture and then track all sales using a defined process (identified, qualified, submitted, won/lost) as this helps determine when to pull out of an opportunity (clearly, the client isn't really committed) and when to make that final push to close the deal (when you have all the right buying signals). This puts you in control of the sales process and prevents you from getting depressed. As you can probably tell, I'm not a natural salesperson.

HERE'S AN IDEA FOR YOU...

Whether it's selling themselves or a company's products, everyone needs to be skilled at this, so it's a good idea to study the sales process and what makes a great salesperson. Speak to the salespeople you know, inside or outside your workplace. Identify what makes them successful and work out what behaviours you need to learn to become good at selling.

45 THE EFFECTS OF VICTORY

Winning might be all that matters but have you considered what the wider implications might be?

DEFINING IDEA...

Victory has a thousand fathers, but defeat is an orphan.

~ JOHN F. KENNEDY, US PRESIDENT

It's a well-known phenomenon that when a football team wins, their male fans experience a significant uplift in their testosterone levels (just ask their partners!). Although temporary, this greatly enhances their overall mood and sense of well-being. Unfortunately, those who support the losing side tend to suffer the opposite effect. In this case, however, the effect lasts much longer and many become quite depressed. What this, of course, tells us is that it's safer to support Chelsea than Scunthorpe United. It also tells us that there are always positive and negative consequences of any victory. Even though he didn't support a major football team, von Clausewitz recognised this. He realised that victory affected the generals and the armies doing the fighting, the state that had been defeated – and interestingly, the battles and wars to be fought in the future.

One area of business illustrating the effects of victory very well is mergers and acquisitions. Long since the preserve of predatory companies and private equity houses, mergers and acquisitions are big business. Although there is meant to be a distinction between an acquisition (in which one company buys another) and a merger (two companies decide to join forces), there are always winners and losers. Most involve power struggles as the CEOs from both companies fight for the top slot. Similar battles also occur throughout the newly created organisation as the two cultures collide: many people lose their jobs, it takes years for the winning company to absorb the loser and lots of time, effort and money is spent on trying to make it work.

Acquisitions have created real problems in the past (for example, when UBS acquired Warburg Dillon Read) and they still cause problems today (Bank of America and Merrill Lynch). I can tell you, it's not much fun to be acquired either. Back in 2000, when I was working for Ernst & Young (E&Y), the management consultancy arm was sold to Cap Gemini for $11 billion. It looked good on paper, but in reality this was a disaster. The two companies were very different: one was US/UK dominant, process-light and collegiate, the other was French, process-heavy and autocratic. The post-acquisition integration was badly handled; stories of Cap and E&Y staff working in the same building, but with separate entrances and teams arguing in front of clients were legend. And the final outcome was... you've guessed it: Cap paid $11 billion for a few thousand laptops as most consultants left. Both companies have gone back to where they were before the acquisition with plenty of shareholder value destroyed in the process. With the majority of mergers and acquisitions failing, surely someone, somewhere, will listen to the advice of von Clausewitz, you might think, wouldn't you?

HERE'S AN IDEA FOR YOU...

Whenever you're in a competitive situation at work, think what the effect of winning will have, both on you and those you are competing with. If you understand the impacts, you'll be able to manage them far more effectively and they won't come as a surprise.

46 STRATEGIC MEANS OF EXPLOITING VICTORY

In battle, true victory only occurs when you follow through and pursue the enemy until they are completely vanquished.

DEFINING IDEA...

Sound trumpets! Let our bloody colours wave! And either victory, or else a grave.

~ WILLIAM SHAKESPEARE, HENRY VI, PART III

If you happen to visit any of the medieval battlefields throughout the UK, you will notice that they all have one thing in common and that's a bloody meadow. Such meadows were so-named because they were where hundreds, even thousands, of combatants were hacked to death as they ran away from the victorious troops of the winning side. In those days no quarter was spared and if you happened to be on the losing side being able to run fast was a core competency. Most were skewered on the ends of the lances of the 'prickers', so-called because their role was to prick the fleeing soldiers. Von Clausewitz would have been pleased: as far as he was concerned, there was little value in victory without the pursuit and annihilation of the enemy.

This brings us back to mergers and acquisitions, and why many fail. It could be argued, of course, that many fail to follow through in the same way that von Clausewitz recommended victorious armies should. In fact, this is not far from the truth. Ultimately, if a merger or acquisition is to succeed there can only be one victor but more critically, the enemy (the acquired or weaker of the two merged companies) has to be crushed in the process. Although there are plenty of acquisitive companies in the world, none compares to Mittal Steel when it comes to following von Clausewitz's advice. Mittal has a commitment to consolidation and globalisation, plus an appetite for risk that puts the fear of God into all its competitors, with good reason too.

During the early years of the twenty-first century, Mittal struggled financially but that didn't prevent it from acquiring new companies. And at a time when everyone believed that steel would remain a regional business, they knew they could become a global giant. Over the next five years, they did just that: they went on an acquisition spree, picking up poor-performing assets and turning them into efficient and profitable operations. Their biggest and boldest move, however, was the hostile bid for Arcelor, their most significant competitor and No. 2 in the global steel market. Mittal recognised that their long-term ambition of being one of a handful of global leaders in the steel industry was at risk and the only way to deal with this was to take out Arcelor, which is exactly what they did. Of course taking over a company is relatively easy, but Mittal understood that true victory means pursuing the enemy until they are vanquished. Their approach to post acquisition was second to none: they replaced existing leaders with their own home grown globetrotting leadership team, who would complete the merger before handing it over to a new team. True victory, in every respect!

HERE'S AN IDEA FOR YOU...

Blowing your own trumpet may not feel like the right thing to do, but in today's highly competitive environment, it is absolutely correct. If you know you do great things and achieve plenty, make sure your boss, and your boss's boss know all about them.

47 THE COMMAND OF HEIGHTS

If you really want to dominate anything, it pays to hold the high ground… and keep it.

DEFINING IDEA...

The Choice: Global Domination or Global Leadership.

– ZBIGNIEW BRZEZINSKI,
US NATIONAL SECURITY ADVISOR

Von Clausewitz loved the word 'dominate' – he felt it had a kind of charm to it (I guess it might have been the Prussian in him). From a military perspective, domination boiled down to one simple thing: holding the high ground. After all, if you want to dominate a battle then you are generally better off being higher up than your enemy; in essence you must command the heights. Von Clausewitz saw three main advantages to this. The first was greater tactical strength. Of course, battles are rarely won by the poor souls who have to fight uphill. If you are on the top of a hill, you will have more options than if you are scaling up it (just ask the Americans who fought the Battle of Iwo Jima). Second, you have greater protection from attack. In other words, it's a lot easier to defend. It's easy to see why many of the castles of England and Wales were impregnable: you almost have a heart attack walking up to them! And finally, you get a wider view. Being elevated allows you to see so much more than from the bottom of a valley and gives you more options. As always, von Clausewitz counters the positives with a few hard truths for the budding commander, not least stating that unless the high ground is exploited, then there really is no reason for having it in the first place. Good point.

Domination is also part and parcel of the market economy. The fundamental nature of business is to beat off all competition and secure the No. 1 slot.

Being the dominant player in a particular market is like holding the high ground in a battle: you can do a greater amount tactically, you can defend more easily and of course you see a lot more because you hold more of the market than anyone else. And if anyone knows how to dominate, it's Microsoft. Having made it big off the back of the PC revolution and the MS-DOS operating system (causing IBM a few problems along the way), Microsoft has used its position of dominance to muscle into everything digital. They have infiltrated so many aspects of our working lives that it's sometimes hard to believe that we could function without them. We use Microsoft products to write, manage our finances, plan projects, prepare sales presentations and send emails.

If that isn't enough, Microsoft plan to dominate other areas such as the games market, cell-phones and internet search engines. Only authorities such as the European Union can stop this global domination. Having tried, it looks as though even they have given up. Microsoft has taken the high ground and it won't be giving this up anytime soon.

HERE'S AN IDEA FOR YOU...

Do you know what markets your company wants to be No. 1 in? If it's already positioned there, what does it do to stay there and how does it exploit its position? If not, what is it doing to dislodge the market leader? Ask some of your business unit leaders – they will be able to tell you. Use the knowledge to see how you can help them achieve their objective.

48 THE KEY TO THE COUNTRY

Sometimes you don't need to capture the whole country to be in control, and sometimes you don't need the whole market to dominate it.

DEFINING IDEA...

Everyone is looking for a unique selling point. Sometimes small touches make an amazing difference.

~ JIM HOSSACK, US AUTO COMMENTATOR

During the eighteenth century, one thing used to excite military planners and leaders more than anything else and that was having the key to the country. Von Clausewitz was clearly less enthralled and somewhat dismissive of those who were, mainly because it had little or no meaning; they had distorted its significance enormously. So, as ever, he decided to put everyone right. His definition was more precise in that he believed that the key to the country was associated with holding a strategically important location from which you could advance into an enemy's territory without major risk. In other words, if you were in control of it, the rest of the country would be easier to attack. Although his argument was mainly associated with the semantics of the expression, it was helpful and made perfect sense. For example, the Normandy beaches, once secured, could be considered the key to France in that the Allies were able to advance from the beachhead without major risk.

From a business perspective, the key to the country could easily be translated into the key to the market. And we could say that the key to the market is associated with winning a strategically important client from which you can expand your market share without risk. The best way to do this is to establish a unique selling point (USP) capable of wowing a potential client and locking them in once they have bought your product or service. Once you have done so, you can use their credential as the means to expand your market share. A good illustration of the key to the market is the Institute of Information Technology (IIT). You may not be aware of this business but they are a software company specialising in combining logistics with operational research and geographical information systems.

Needless to say, IIT employs some highly intelligent individuals, who can solve the type of complex problems that would make most others pass out. They use their expertise to optimise routes for the businesses with whom they work, saving skip loads of money in the process. It is this ability to take work out of the system that is their unique selling point and they have been able to capture the key to the waste business market by securing the three largest waste companies in North America. Although the market has a number of players and there are plenty of opportunities to go around, it has been IIT's ability to dislodge incumbents and retain these large clients that has established the beachhead from which they can expand. IIT may not choose to work for every waste company in North America, but they probably could. That's the advantage of having the key to the country: it gives you options.

HERE'S AN IDEA FOR YOU...

Can you identify your company's unique selling points (USPs)? Could you write them down without giving too much thought to it? What is it that you and your team do to reinforce the USPs? Do you think you could contribute more?

49 TYPES OF RESISTANCE

Used effectively, resistance can be a perfect way to stop anything in its tracks – invading armies, major projects and even business change.

DEFINING IDEA...

I assess the power of a will by how much resistance, pain, torture it endures and knows how to turn to its advantage.

~ FRIEDRICH NIETZSCHE. GERMAN PHILOSOPHER

When faced with an enemy intent on attacking you, it's generally a good idea to be in a position to defend your country. However, von Clausewitz points out that there were a number of options available to the defending nation. They could attack the enemy as soon as they entered their field of operations or wait until the enemy was near their frontier and attack them before they were battle-ready; they could wait until they had actually crossed their border or withdraw into the interior of the country and resist there. Although all were useful strategies, the last one was often the most effective because the enemy would either get bored and go away, or be so weakened by the need to protect the territory they had captured along the way that they would be easy pickings when it came to counterattack.

The most common resistance experienced in the corporate world is associated with organisational change. Irrespective of what the experts might say, most of us would be content if things never changed at all. However, no markets stay the same for long so although we might not want to change, in most cases we must do so. Of course that does not make it any easier. A couple of years ago I was involved with a major transformation programme in North America. It was a big undertaking and involved every part of the company.

One key element involved capturing, cleaning and enhancing vast amounts of operational data on which the whole programme and benefits depended. The guy given the job really wasn't interested and spent all his energy finding ways not to do the work he had volunteered to do. I spent hours helping him to understand the criticality of his role, developed plans to deliver his part of the programme and even brokered meetings between all the key stakeholders. Whatever I did, he threw up yet another barrier, however.

There are three ways to address such resistance. The first is to use what is known as the empirical-rational approach. This assumes we are all rational and driven by self-interest, that if the right information is given to us, we will see the wisdom in the change and go along with it. The next is the normative-re-educative approach, which assumes change is values-based and as such needs to consider everyone's opinions. In this instance, success relies on the collective involvement of all stakeholders to arrive at a solution that satisfies all players. The third is the power-coercive approach. Here, it doesn't matter a hoot if you don't like the change, it's a case of shut-up or ship-out. Coming back to our friend in North America, I am still waiting to hear if he has received his pink slip.

HERE'S AN IDEA FOR YOU...

How does your business tackle resistance to change? Is it a case of steamrollering the change through, or does it adopt a more persuasive approach? What does this tell you about how change is managed in your business? More importantly, how you would tackle resistance in your team?

50 THE CHARACTER OF STRATEGIC DEFENCE

Merely defending your position is not enough, you have to be prepared to strike back and seize back the advantage.

DEFINING IDEA...

Our opponent is our helper.

– EDMUND BURKE, STATESMAN AND WRITER

Von Clausewitz's view of defence is not a simple case of holding your enemy at bay; it has to be so much more as he clearly states, 'A sudden powerful transition to the offensive – the flashing sword of vengeance – is the greatest moment for the defense. If it is not in the commander's mind from the start, or rather if it is not an integral part of his idea of defense, he will never be persuaded of the superiority of the defensive form; all he will see is how much of the enemy's resources he can destroy or capture.' Here, there is an explicit assumption that although the aggressor calls for the defender to defend, it is in the defender's best interests to always be looking for the counterstrike. Von Clausewitz makes it clear that the advantage does not always lie with those who make the first move. As someone who is a keen fencer, I can attest to the immense satisfaction that comes with a good parry quarte riposte!

In 2001, despite having a near 40% share of the silicon market, Dow Corning was under increasing pressure from low-cost competitors. Although it would have been simple to defend their market by reducing prices, they decided to adopt a dual strategy which would both allow them to maintain their premium services while taking the low-cost competition head-on – the strategic defence.

In 2003, after two years of analysis, carefully segmenting its market and approaching potential customers, Dow launched Xiameter, its low-cost business. Compared with Dow Corning, which sells 7,000 products, Xiameter offers just 350 and focuses exclusively on those products which face intense competition, both from the low-cost entrants as well as Dow itself. Xiameter's products are 20% cheaper than Dow's and come without any additional services. Dow also adopted every trick of the low-cost provider by extending delivery times, only delivering full truck, tank or pallet loads of goods, charging for non-web ordered products, offering reduced credit terms and charging for rush orders and cancellations. The biggest advantage has been in the set-up and running costs, minimised through the ability to use idle production lines within the existing manufacturing plants. This approach has not only helped bolster Dow's profits (going from a $28 m loss in 2001 to $500 m profit in 2005), but it has also helped its customers appreciate the additional benefits that Dow brings to the market, which in turn has protected its market share and allowed the company to maintain its premium prices.

Dow's response was a masterstroke and demonstrates the need to consider what your competitors tell you about your own business model. Although it is often tempting to dismiss new entrants and respond without thinking, it pays to keep your powder dry and establish a powerful response.

HERE'S AN IDEA FOR YOU...

With your team, carry out a SWOT analysis of your business. Seek to understand its strengths, its weaknesses (the internal factors), as well as the market opportunities and threats (the external factors). Is there anything you and your team could do to help maximise the strengths, minimise the weaknesses, exploit the opportunities and counter the threats? Once you have finished, develop an action plan to address the points raised.

51 RETREAT AFTER A LOST BATTLE

Retreating after a battle has been lost is no easy feat and requires careful planning to limit further losses; the same is true when pulling out of an overseas market.

DEFINING IDEA...

Who is sure of their own motives can in confidence advance or retreat.

~ JOHANN WOLFGANG VON GOETHE, GERMAN PLAYWRIGHT

When an army loses a battle its manpower is severely depleted and morale is usually in tatters, that much is clear. But as von Clausewitz points out, unless the army is reinforced or manages to hide behind the walls of a fortress, its prospects for survival are not great. However, if it can retreat in an orderly fashion, protected by a strong rearguard action; can use the terrain to their advantage and be bold enough to harry the enemy as it makes its escape, it will live to fight another day. Stopping a rout is never easy, but it is possible and some of the best examples come from World War I and II, such as the battle of the Marne (August 1914), when a well-executed rearguard action by the British Expeditionary Force stopped the German advance in its tracks and in May to June 1940, when Allied troops were evacuated from Dunkirk. In both cases, careful planning limited potential losses.

No doubt globalisation has been a boon to those companies wishing to expand beyond their home territories. In particular, those who recognised the importance of tailoring their brands to local markets have done especially well; think Coca-Cola and McDonalds. However, sometimes it's necessary to pull out of a foreign market because it's not profitable enough or having an overseas presence no longer forms a key part of strategy. In such cases it is necessary to manage the withdrawal carefully. Like many retailers, including Sainsbury's and Tesco, Marks & Spencer sees the value in expanding their brand to other parts of the world. Their move into overseas markets started in Western Europe in 1975. Since then they launched stores in Eastern Europe, the Middle East and China. For a time they did pretty well, even initiating a further £2 billion expansion into overseas markets in 1998. However, in 2001, when the whole company was suffering very badly, they decided to pull out of their Western European operations to concentrate on their struggling UK business. Although the decision was not taken lightly, all 38 branches in continental Europe, including the flagship stores in Paris, Barcelona, Madrid and Cologne, were closed (with some 3,400 job losses). No doubt their exit was carefully planned to ensure the businesses were sold off if they could be, but their reputation suffered badly because of French reaction to the closures. French workers were particularly upset and, believing they were being singled out for job cuts, they took to the streets. Although some of the reputational damage was repaired when Marks & Spencer sold the stores to the Galeries Lafayette chain, clearly even in retreat, you cannot plan for everything.

HERE'S AN IDEA FOR YOU...

All of us fail from time to time and although it is often an unpleasant experience, it can be a powerful learning tool, too. If you have failed at something, don't try and blame someone else or circumstances, seek to understand your role in the failure and what you can learn from the process to avoid making the same mistake again.

52 RETREAT TO THE INTERIOR OF THE COUNTRY

One of the best forms of defence is to retreat into the interior of the country. Paradoxically, in today's markets, the best form of attack is to retreat to your core competencies.

DEFINING IDEA...

Core competencies are the source of competitive advantage.

– GARY HAMEL AND C.K. PRAHALAD, MANAGEMENT GURUS

When under attack from an enemy, one of the options open is to retreat deep into your home territory. This type of defence has always been the preferred response of the Russians. When combined with a scorched earth policy, in which anything useful to the attacking forces was destroyed or burnt, they were unbeatable; just ask Napoleon or Hitler. As von Clausewitz points out, this approach to the defence of a nation destroyed the enemy not so much by the sword as by his own exertions. There are a number of reasons for this. First, the invader found it harder to supply and billet their troops. Second, progress was slower the deeper they went into their enemy's territory, especially if they had a large army. Finally, the strategic and tactical overhead increases significantly to the point where troop movements ground to a halt due to the time lag between intelligence reaching the command post and new orders being issued. All in all, it was a great tactical move.

There is an interesting organisational behaviour associated with a company's core competencies that tends to follow a period of success: when times are good and companies are awash with extra cash, they will often expand outside their main markets. They tend to do so because of the belief that if they are successful in one sector, they can be equally successful in another. Of course this is rarely the case. In 1968, Xerox dominated the photocopier business, holding something like 80% of the market. The new CEO, Peter McColough, believed that Xerox could also dominate the newly minted electronic storage market (which became the computing market). It started off very well and soon Xerox was way ahead of IBM and Apple; the first to develop many of the things we now associate with personal computing, like the graphical user interface, mouse, laser printer and even the computer itself. However, in the process Xerox abandoned the core competencies, which made it such a great photocopier business. They started to ignore their customers and no longer made products they wanted; they abandoned their innovative business model, which made their copiers such an attractive proposition and they failed to protect their intellectual property. Sure, they did some wonderful things but had they stuck to their core competencies, this book might have been written on a Xerox computer, not an IBM.

I'm a great fan of sticking to the knitting and my advice to anyone is to listen to von Clausewitz and retreat to the interior of the country. In other words, stick to what you are good at and known for. Let those wishing to emulate you wear themselves down so that you don't have to.

HERE'S AN IDEA FOR YOU...

What are your company's core competencies? Can you list them and do you fully understand what they mean to your organisation's success? Ask some or all of the senior team; they ought to know. Ideally, there should be a clear link between the core competencies and the success of the products or services your organisation sells.

INDEX

A

ABB, 24
Abbott, John, 53
acquisitions, 91–2, 93–4
Advance Corp, 61, 63
After Action Review (AAR), 82
Agincourt, 31, 73
Allen, George, 61
América Móvil, 10
American Express, 72
American Productivity and Quality Center
      (APQC), 30
analysis, 9–10, 81–2, 85–6
Apple, 74
Apprentice, The (tv programme), 71–2
Arcelor, 94
armies
      After Action Review (AAR), 82
      billets, 35
      communications, 23, 25
      composition and deployment,
            16, 19, 63
            technical innovation and, 21
            unification, in time, 67
      routine and discipline, 29
      strategic and tactical planning, 15, 67
      supply lines, 27
      see also battles; war
Artillery, 19

B

banking sector, 12, 20, 54, 67–8, 84
Bannister, Roger, 47
Bannockburn, Battle of, 55
Barnevik, Percy, 23
battles
      Agincourt, 31, 73

Bannockburn, 55
Brécourt Manor, 57
Dunkirk, 103
Khartoum, 65
Marne, 103
Normandy, 97
Waterloo, 31
see also armies; war
Bell, Alexander Graham, 25
Bernard, Claude, 3
Berra, Yogi, 7
Blitzkrieg strategy, 51
Branson, Richard, 40
Brezezinski, Zbigniew, 95
BRIC economies, 10
British Airways, 20, 59–60
British Gas, 14
Burke, Edmund, 101
business *see* company adaptability; company
      identity; company strategy; company
      structure and function

C

Cap Gemini, 92
car manufacturers, 32, 73–4
Cavalry, 19, 21
'cave' environment, 62
CEOs (Chief Executive Officers)
      see leadership
change, 16, 21, 76
      company adaptability, 22, 51–2, 60
      organisational, 99–100, 100
      in working environment, 36
Chapman, George, 43
Child Support Agency, 88
Chrysler, Walter, 50
CNOOC, 10

commerce *see* company adaptability;
company identity; company strategy;
company structure and function
communication, 23, 25–6, 26
culture and, 53–4
with suppliers, 28
company adaptability, 22, 51–2, 60
company identity, 24
company strategy
attack, 59–60, 65–6, 66
boldness, 45–6
business operations and, 57–8, 58, 67–8
cunning, 49–50, 50
financial reserves, 69–70, 70
general surveys, 17–18, 18
market concentration, 65–6
marketing, 31–2, 32, 50, 62
concentration, 65–6
competitive advantage, 74, 74, 95–6,
96, 101–2
defensive barriers to entry, 33–4, 34
sales and, 89–90, 90, 97–8
saturation, 78
withdrawal, 103–4
planning, 79–80, 80
project management, 87–8, 88
retreat to core competencies, 105–6
company structure and function, 20, 20
communications and, 25–6
control of operations, 23–4, 57–8
innovation and, 22, 25–6, 62
R&D and production, 61–2
organisational change, 99–100, 100
standardised processes, 29–30
competitive and comparative advantage,
73–4, 74
Confucius, 37
consultancy firms, 18, 63–4, 64, 92
core competencies, 105–6, 106
core values, 54
corruption, 38
Costco, 74
courage, 55
Credit Crunch (2009), 8, 44, 52
effects of, 60, 69–70
critical analysis, 81–2
CS90 project, 84
culture, organisational, 53–4
cunning, 49–50
customer focus, 74
customer loyalty schemes, 76

D

decision-making, 12, 77, 77, 77–8, 78, 82
Denver City airport, 88
Discipline of Market Leaders, The, 74
domination, 95–6
Dow Corning, 101–2
Drucker, Peter, 31
dynamic law of war, 77

E

Edison, Thomas, 15, 47–8
egotism, 41–2, 42
Eiffel Tower, 49–50
email, 26
Embraer, 10
Emerson, Ralph Waldo, 63
emotional intelligence, 55–6
employees *see* working life
environment, 35–6
Ernst & Young, 54, 92
esprit de corps, 53–4
Euwe, Max, 57

F

fear, 55
financial reserves, 69–70, 70
Five Forces model, 34
fortresses, 33–4
friction, 83–4

G

games consoles, 77–8
Gates, Bill, 21
GE (General Electric), 15–16, 40
general surveys, 17–18, 18
genius, 39–40
Gilpin, Bernard, 75
Gingrich, Newt, 47
globalisation, 12, 24, 103
acquisitions and, 94
CS90 project, 84
Goethe, Johann Wolfgang von, 103
government
departments, 58
interference, 14, 34

H

Hamel, Gary, 105
Hazlitt, William, 49
Higginson, Thomas, 11
historical examples, four key uses, 9–10
Hitchcock, Alfred, 71
Hitler, Adolf, 41
Hossack, Jim, 97
HR (human resources), 4, 20, 40
    core values, 54
Human Relations movement, 3

I

IBM, 22
Infantry, 19, 21
information, 85–6
information technology (IT), 12, 26
innovation, 21–2, 78
    in communications, 25–6
Institute of Information Technology
    (IIT), 98
Intel, 26
investment analysts, 69
investment banks, 20
Isochron, 80

J

Jack Ma, 13
Jobs, Steve, 40
Johnson, Samuel, 17, 87
Johnson & Johnson, 74
Johnson, Joss, 72
Jones, John Paul, 51

K

Kakuzo Okakaura, 15
Kennedy, John F. 91
Kentuck Fried Chicken, 48
Khartoum, Battle of, 65
Kiam, Victor, 33
Kohlberg, Kravis & Roberts (KKR), 72

L

leadership
    decision-making, 12, 77–8, 82
    egotism, 41–2
    priorities, 68
    responsibilities, 6, 37–8, 38, 59–60

    ruthlessness, 71–2
learning, 5–6, 6
    analysis and, 81–2
    historical examples, 9–10
    how your business works, 20, 22, 58
    theory as a guide, 7–8
Lexus cars, 32
Lloyd Wright, Frank, 81
Long Term Capital Management, 44
Louis XIV, 35

M

Mackay, Harvey, 89
Madoff, Bernie, 38
maintenance and supply, 27–8
management theory, 3
marketing, 50, 62
    sales and, 89–90, 90, 97–8
markets, 31–2, 32
    concentration, 65–6
    competitive advantage in, 74, 74, 95–6,
        96, 101–2
    defensive barriers to entry, 33–4, 34
    saturation, 78
    withdrawal from, 103–4
Marks & Spencer, 104
Massechusetts Institute of Technology
    (MIT), 30
Master of Business Administration (MBA)
    programmes, 7–8
McColough, Peter, 106
McKinsey & Company, 18
Meredith, Owen, 39
mergers and acquisitions, 91–2, 93–4
Microsoft, 20, 22, 52, 78, 96
military genius, 39
Mittal Steel, 93–4
Mittal, Lakshmi, 40
monopolies, 14
moral factors, 37–8
Murdock, Mike, 29

N

Nabisco, 72
Naisbitt, John, 27
Napoleon Bonaparte, 15, 40, 41
Netscape, 52
Neuro-linguistic Programming (NLP), 56
Nietzsche, Friedrich, 99
Nintendo, 78

Nixon, Richard, 79

O

O'Leary, Michael, 45–6
office space, 35–6
On War, 1–2, 67
Ordnance Survey, 61
organisational change, 99–100
organisational culture, 53–4

P

patents, 34
Patton, General George S., 45
people-handling skills, 4
performance, 83–4
perseverance, 47–8, 48
planning, 79–80, 80
    from theory to action, 83–4, 84
Plato, 55
Player, Gary, 83
Polaroid, 52
political aims, 13–14, 14
    moral corruption and, 38
political purpose of war, 79
Porter, Michael, 34
Prahalad, C.K., 105
problem solving, 8
processes, 29–30, 30
    risk management, 43–4, 44
Proctor & Gamble (P&G), 28, 62
product leadership, 74
production, 61–2
project management, 87–8, 88

R

Ray, Lisa, 69
reports, 10, 86
research and development (R&D), 61–2
Reserve, 69
resistance to change, 99–100, 100
resources, superiority of, 75–6
retail sector, 28
Retail Supply Chain Certification
Programme, 28
retreat, 103, 105
risk management, 43–4, 44, 52
Roosevelt, Theodore, 77
routine, 29–30
Royal Engineers, 79

ruthlessness, 71–2, 72
Ryanair, 45–6, 74

S

SAB Miller, 10
Sadia, 10
sales, 89–90, 90, 97–8
    unique selling point (USP), 98, 98
Santayana, George, 9
scientific management, 3
self-assertion, 45–6, 46, 59–60, 94
    ruthlessness and, 71–2
Semco, 4
Semler, Ricardo, 4
Seneca, 59
Severance, Craig, 50
Shakespeare, William, 93
Shearson Lehman Hutton, 72
Shula, Don, 67
skyscraper race, 50
Socrates, 5
Sony, 78
Sorrell, Sir Martin, 63
Starbucks, 65–6
start-up businesses, 34
steel industry, 94
strategic planning see company strategy
success and failure, 87–8, 88, 104
Sugar, Sir Alan, 63, 71
supermarket wars, 75–6
supply, 27–8
surprise, 51–2, 52
SWOT analysis, 102
systems theory, 11–12

T

Tata Consultancy Services, 10
terrain, 31–2
Tesco, 75–6
theory as a guide, 7–8
Thermopylae, 31
Thirty Years War, 27
Townsend, Robert, 41
Toyota, 32
Treacy, Michael, 74
Tuck Business School (USA), 7

U

unique selling point (USP), 98, 98
Untouchables, The (film), 48

V

victory, 91–2
    and follow-up, 93–4
Vietnam War, 82
virtual stores, 62
von Clausewitz, Carl, 1–2, 57, 81, 95

W

Wal-Mart, 12, 27–8
Walsh, Willie, 59–60
war
    and the use of cunning, 49
    as an act of human intercourse, 3–4
    as part of wide system, 11–12
    'bigger picture general survey', 17
    changing nature of, 27
    defence, 99, 101
        and retreat, 103, 105
    defensive fortresses, 33
    duration of engagement, 89
    dynamic law of, 77
    emotions of, 55, 91
    friction, 83
    intelligence, 85
    knowledge and application, 5–6
    likelihood of success, 87
    military genius, 39
    moral spirit of, 37–8, 59
    purpose and objective, 79
    strategic thinking, 51, 57, 65
        and tactics, 61, 69, 75
            superiority of numbers, 73
    terrain, 31–2
    victory, 91–2
    see also armies; battles
War of the Roses, 13
Waterloo, 31
Welch, Jack, 16, 40, 73
Westpac, 84
Wilson, Woodrow, 25, 85
Wiersema, Fred, 74
Wii, 78
working life, 36
    emotions of, 56, 92
    mergers and acquisitions, 91–2
    working space, 35–6
World War I, 11, 53
    battle of Marne, 103
World War II, 51, 53
    assault on Brécourt Manor, 57
    Dunkirk, 103
    Normandy invasion, 97

X

Xerox, 105–6
Xiameter, 102